Building

Fans, Fame and Wealth

The 18 Revenue Streams of Music

By

Ed Wimp

Wimp Entertainment
Orlando, Florida

Building Fans, Fame and Wealth…
The 18 Revenue Streams of Music
© 2016 by Ed Wimp

ISBN-10: 0-692-73913-0
ISBN-13: 978-0-692-73913-6

Library of Congress Control Number: 2016911243

Cover Design: J. L. Woodson - www.jlwoodson.com
Interior Book Design: Lissa Woodson - www.macrompg.com

Distributed by Ingram Book Group
Ed Wimp trade paperback edition August 2016
10 9 8 7 6 5 4 3 2 1
Manufactured and printed in the United States of America

For information regarding discounts for bulk purchases, please contact us at info@edwimp.com

Many thanks to: Jabari McDavid, Monroe Hart, Tom Drahozal, Dalyn Drown, Wilbert Terrell, Verdine White, Philip Bailey, Ralph Johnson, Rakim Mayers and the many others who have helped direct my career thus far. I would also like to extend a special thank you to Blythe Whitinger, as well as to my loving parents, Greta Pope Wimp and Edward L. Wimp.

Table of Contents

HOW TO MAKE MONEY IN MUSIC:
The 18 Revenue Streams of Music

Table of Contents *(continued)*

Introduction

I have long thought of the term "music industry" as ironic. To think that creative, artistic individuals could have a place in the serious world of business seems akin to the relationship between oil and water. The drastic contrast that I perceived between music and business attracted me to the industry at a very young age. I have been a musician for most of my life, starting out as a violinist at age 5, transitioning to trumpet at 9 and transitioning yet again to guitar at 14. Music has always been an important part of my life, as my mother and grandmother both had professional careers as vocalists. I had an opportunity to see and experience the importance of music in society. The musical genre doesn't matter. It is clear that people are dramatically affected by music. We can all relate specific songs to memorable events or times in our lives. Every time that I hear Green Day's "When September Ends," I think about the summer between my 9th and 10th grade years and the wonderful friends that shared that summer with me, many of whom are still my friends today. I'm sure that you have memories like that as well. Music is important to all of us.

Through Building Fans, Fame and Wealth, I will share with you some of the things that I have learned through observation and through hands on experience in the music industry. I have been very fortunate to have wonderful mentors and it is important to me to "pay it forward."

Background

I was privileged to be able to travel the world and witness the music business first hand as I watched my mother's singing career. I fell in love with the industry. The music industry is unique in the fact that everyone involved is passionate about music in some way or another. For example, if you worked in another industry, you may or may not be passionate about the company's product, but you continue to work there because the job 'pays the bills.' However, individuals working in the music industry are in the industry for a reason other than the incentive of money. They either love the music, the travel, the lifestyle, the clout, the production, etc., or they love all of the above. With the stringent demands of a career in the music industry, it is important to have a strong passion for the music and for the industry. If the demands ever become overwhelming, remember why you pursued a career in music. You pursued it for the love of the music.

The bulk of my professional experience has been in the area of artist management and tour management. One of the biggest challenges of working in management is bringing organization to the creative, busy lives of musicians. Managing finances, branding, marketing and scheduling is often difficult for musicians because their talents and special skills lie more in the artistic space. In addition, their efforts are spent creating their art, so they don't have the time to manage the day-to-day operational aspects of their career.

In order to address the many management needs of a successful artist, you would need the services of several different types of managers.

Understanding the Role of the Management Team

The Management Team

There are many types of managers in the music industry. The more established the act, the more managers they are likely to have for different roles. The basic general management roles include a business manager, music manager, road manager, tour manager, production manager, and technical manager. I will give a brief breakdown of the different management roles:

Business Manager:

A "business manager" is good with numbers and is often an accountant. It is up to this person to manage the revenue and expenses of the business. They will assure that all payment is collected and accounted for. This person will pay the lead musicians, background musicians, crew, tour management, venue, etc. They will also make sure that taxes are paid and that all of the artist's finances are in order. The business manager might also connect the artist with quality investment professionals to preserve and grow their wealth.

Music Manager:

The "music manager", or "artist manager" advises the talent on all aspects on their career. They will help the artist to reach the audience and assist the artist with recording, publishing, merchandising, and touring opportunities. The music manager also advises on sponsorships, branding, and licensing. The music manager faces outward, seeking opportunities and collaborations with companies and other artists.

Road Manager:

The "road manager" tends to logistics while on tour. Their tasks lie heavily in making sure that everything that happens on the road is according to contract. This manager ensures that payments are made on time. The road manager allows the artist to focus solely on the performance, on appearances, and on pleasing the fans. The road manager is in communication with promoters, agents, sponsors, and other personnel to assure that everything runs smoothly.

Tour Manager:

Large tours require a "tour manager." The tour manager role sometimes appears to overlap with the role of road manager. However, because there are so many more details to handle on large tours, more people are needed to ensure that things run smoothly. The tour manager coordinates everything on the tour, including the activities of the road manager. The tour manager is in charge of the bigger picture (the entire tour), instead of tending to everyday activities, which is what the road manager does. A tour manager will be key in planning merchandising, tour routing, catering, hospitality, etc.

Production Manager:

"Production managers" are generally a luxury of larger tours for major artists. They will work in tandem with tour managers and coordinate logistics such as renting sound, video, lighting, trucking logistics, and coordinating scheduling for touring crew and local venue crew.

Technical Manager:

The "technical manager" is in charge of set construction, set design and other technicalities that are a part of the actual performance. They will work closely with the production manager.

Typically, the larger the tour, the more specialized the management roles will be. On small tours, there might be only one manager that handles all responsibilities. However, on large tours, these roles need to be split up in order to operate most efficiently.

Management is not a field that you can learn by just reading a book. To really get a feel for management, it must be experienced. A large part of any manager's job involves managing the human resources of the organization. All members of the tour must be made clear on exactly what their job entails. Everyone should be made to feel valuable to the organization. This will help personnel to be successful at their job. Feeling "valued" is important to all of us. Understanding different personality types and developing good problem-solving skills is very important. In the music industry, these problem-solving skills must often be employed in high-pressure situations when there are tens of thousands of people in the audience waiting for a concert. Composure is an essential attribute for anyone seeking to work in the field of entertainment management. Grace under pressure!

A CASE STUDY

A few years ago, I was in Pittsburgh with an act for which I was tour manager. We had done a sold-out performance in New York the night before. After the show in New York, everyone except for the lead singer got on the busses and headed to Pittsburgh. The lead singer opted to go to his girlfriend's house for the night and fly to Pittsburgh the next day with his bodyguard. The lead singer was to arrive in Pittsburg in plenty of time for the act to go onstage for their highly anticipated performance at 8:00 p.m. At about 3:00 p.m., we received a phone call from the lead singer and his bodyguard saying that he had forgotten his driver's license at his girlfriend's house and was not able to get through security at the airport. They were going to miss the flight! This was without a doubt the biggest catastrophe of my professional career at that point. We had a sold out concert at the First Niagara Pavilion with 23,000 fans in the audience who were all there to see the artist that had just called me to say that there was a chance that he wouldn't make it! At that moment, I could have locked myself in my bunk on the bus and not emerged until we were well out of the Pittsburgh city limits, but I had to put on my game face and make something work with our team.

As it turned out, the artist was able to go back to his girlfriend's, get his ID, and board a flight that was to land in Pittsburgh at 8:10. So great!! He will make it to Pittsburgh at 8:10, but there was still one problem… his set started at 8:00! As you might imagine, my team and I endured a lot of backlash from the venue and the afternoon was spent keeping everyone as calm as possible. Once 8 o'clock came around, we decided to send the rest of the band out on stage as we called for police escorts to aid in getting the lead singer from the airport to the venue in record time. All said and done, he was there by 8:40, which was enough time to give the audience a little less than an hour of his live performance. It was a whirlwind day but we thought on our feet, we did everything we could and we pulled it off.

LESSON LEARNED:

We implemented new regulations to keep this kind of thing from happening again. Management in any field is about anticipating problems, solving problems, leading teams, and executing the tasks necessary to accomplish your goal, while remaining as calm as possible. Grace under pressure! The artist's brand and reputation are at stake. Failure is not an option, as it could do irreparable damage to the artist's future and to the manager's future. The consequences of not accomplishing the goal could have a hugely detrimental impact on everyone involved.

The Artist Manager and the Contract

The phrase "music business" can be construed as an oxymoron. Suggesting that art is to be branded and sold for monetary gain is difficult for some to digest. The role of an artist manager is to bridge the gap between creativity and business. This is a prime example of "specialization of labor". The artist is left to perfect and execute their craft, while the manager is left to handle what they do best, which is making a profit.

It is my personal philosophy that a manager is not needed until the day-to-day business tasks are impeding the creative process of making music. However, if the artist is really challenged where business is concerned, finding a manager early on may be in the best interest of the artist.

The main goal of the artist manager is to represent the interests of the artist. The artist manager will work with the artist to develop the artist's brand. They will shop content to various outlets in the music industry including, radio, retail, publicity, blogs, distributors, record labels, etc.

A manager should either be well connected, or have a very strong passion and desire for the success of the artist's business. Preferably, the manager would have both…great contacts as well as a passion for the artist's business. The manager is responsible for assembling a strong team that will handle all of the artist's business needs and lead to lots of work and good income for the artist and for everyone involved.

It is important to do your research on a prospective manager in order to ensure that they have similar values to yours and that they have had a good track record with previous clients. Ask around and get second opinions.

The Contract

Once you have selected an artist manager that is a good fit for your business, it is time to enter into a contract. Manager fees vary greatly, but most earn a commission on the net or gross income of the artist. Reasonable management contracts can allow the manager to earn up to 20% of the gross income – including record royalties, merchandising, touring, publishing income, etc.

Often, there will be a "sunset clause" in the contract, which will specify the declining payments that the manager will receive in the event that the two parties cease to work together. This allows the manager to still earn payments for a few years from the work that he/she did while the two parties were in a working relationship.

It is important to have an entertainment business attorney review the contract before signing. When negotiating a contract with a manager, the artist should have an attorney, separate from that of the manager. Acquiring proper legal counsel protects the artist's interests.

The Electronic Press Kit

As a manager, the first thing I do when I sign a new artist is to make sure that they have a professional "electronic press kit." An electronic press kit, or an "EPK", is a commonly used document that is sent to clubs, music industry professionals, media, or anybody that the musician is interested in working with. Think of an electronic press kit as a resume for musicians.

The EPK is made up of the following components:

-Contact Information (Manger's email and phone info, artist's website)
-Biography (Brief paragraph(s) outlining the artist's career accomplishments)

-Photographs

-Testimonials (from past clients and/or fans)

-Press Coverage (Any articles, written interviews, audio or video interviews)

-Show Information (listing of upcoming shows or notable past shows)

-Links to Content (music video, music)

The biography should be informative but brief. The music should be highlighted in the most succinct way possible, and mention the artists accomplishments.

Make sure that all links that are provided work properly. And do not provide links to all of the content. Instead, provide links to the best three songs, and the best music video.

Images are more important than many think. It is worth the investment to do a photo shoot that will help to give the act a professional look. Clients will be more willing to work with the artist if the artist looks and sounds professional.

Include quotes from well-respected members of the music industry and include links to any press coverage that you have.

Mention past shows that the artist has done. When planning a tour and attempting to book a show at a venue in a city they have performed in before, be sure to mention the previous venue they played in that city and the fan turnout.

An electronic press kit should look professional and be easy to navigate. Make it as easy as possible for the reader to locate all content.

HOW TO MAKE MONEY IN MUSIC:
The 18 Revenue Streams of Music

I am a big supporter of setting S.M.A.R.T. goals, which is an acronym for Smart, Measurable, Achievable, Relevant, and Time Measured. When reading through the various streams of revenue that I have outlined, be sure to keep in mind your personal S.M.A.R.T. goals for each revenue stream. By keeping your efforts centered around your goals, you can better gauge your progress. Many people that are new to the music industry think that money can only be made through live performances and selling CD's. I have come up with eighteen different revenue streams that musicians have the capability of exploiting. They are not in order of importance:

1. Live Shows

2. Physical Merchandise

3. Digital Merchandise

4. CD Sales

5. Vinyl Sales

6. Digital Music Sales

7. Streaming

8. Songwriting

9. Licensing

10. Publishing Royalties

11. Digital Royalties

12. Live Performance Royalties

13. Session Work/Features

14. Sponsorships

15. Crowdfunding

16. YouTube

17. Cover Gigs

18. Music Lessons/Workshops

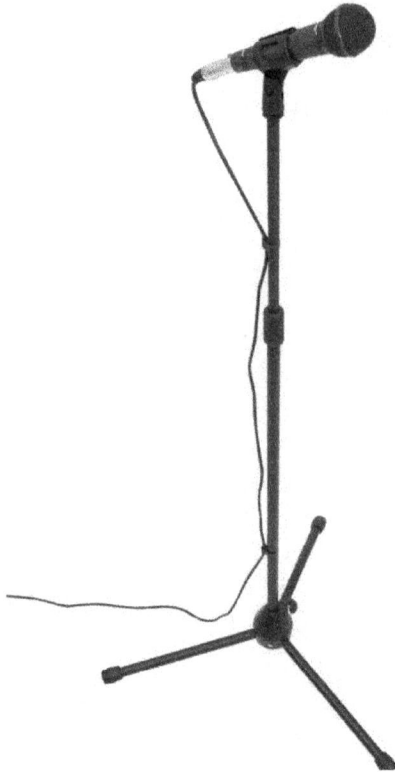

Chapter 1

LIVE SHOWS

The Preparation

Live performances have been a consistent way for musicians to make money since people have been playing music. The live performance can be a very fruitful revenue stream for musicians if the event is executed correctly.

Musicians will often work with a promoter when they are doing a show at a venue. A Concert Promoter can either work on behalf of a band, or a venue. When working on behalf of the band, the promoter's responsibility is to find locations for the band to play. In addition, their job is to promote the artist and the concert. Concert promoters serve as a key component in the booking and preparation of many live performances. The information I am going to give you is useful for both musicians that will be dealing with promoters, and for those that would like to begin promoting concerts.

Lineup:

First things first! The promoter will need to research and select a venue to hold the event. The Concert Promoter must also select and book acts to perform. When determining the venue, it is important to first analyze the target demographic that will be coming to the event. For example, if this is going to be a hip-hop show, calling the local orchestra hall to suggest this concert may not be feasible. It is best to target reputable venues that typically host the kind of event that you plan to do. Once a suitable venue has been selected, the Concert Promoter should contact the venue, negotiate terms of the agreement and book a date to hold the event.

There will then need to be a bill, or a "lineup" of artists. When booking the talent, the concert promoter will need to make sure that the acts being considered for the concert make sense playing together in the same show. At the end of the day, the objective is to create value for the consumer. Featuring a smattering of many genres on the bill may run the risk of completely missing every demographic. Think about when a major tour comes to town, the bands or artists always appeal to a similar demographic. For example, the Drake vs. Lil Wayne tour featured two artists, Drake and Lil Wayne. They appeal to a very similar demographic. An individual may not be a big enough Drake fan to come out to see just him, but when the value of Lil Wayne is added, the concert is suddenly worth the price of a ticket.

The Offer:

There are different ways of striking a monetary agreement with a Concert Promoter. I will highlight the most common methods below:

- Promoter Profit Deal: This type of deal is very typical. The promoter, will budget out the event expenses and then the artist will add the promoter expense on top of the overhead expenses as the promoter profit expense. When your event clears your breakeven point (expenses including promoter profit), you then split the net 85%/15% (tour/promoter). So for example, if the expenses of an event accumulate to $60,000 and the promoter is going to build in an extra $10,000 into the overhead for his/her profit, the breakeven point will be $70,000. If the event returns $100,000 in gross profit, the net profit of the event will be $30,000. Therefore, with an 85/15 split, the band will walk away with $25,500 (30,000 x .85) and the promoter will walk away with 14,400 (30,000 x .15=$4,500) ($4,500 + $10,000=$14,500). The promoter contracts with the venue and agrees to pay all other expenses. The Promoter Profit Deal provides increased incentive for the promoter to take the risk necessary to bring the event to fruition.

- Gross Split Deal: In a gross split deal, the artist and promoter split the money from ticket sales with no deductions. You can modify this by doing a gross split AFTER specific expenses, however this gets to be a hard sell if the split is a bit high.

-

-   Vs. Deal: Versus deals mean that you will offer one thing or another thing depending on specific variables. For instance, "$500 vs. 50% of gross" would mean that you are offering $500 or 50% of the gross ticket sales. For example, with a "$500 or 50% of gross" deal, if the talent brings in $2000 of gross profit, the talent would receive $1000 ($2000 x .5=$1000) ($1000>$500). If the gross profit is $800, the talent would receive the $500. ($800 x .5=$400) ($400<$500). You can specify which ever is higher or lower, you can determine a gross to be after specific expenses, etc. etc. These deals can get quite complex very quickly.

-   Net Split Deal: Net splits are exactly what they sound like. The artist gets paid out a specific percentage of net. The net is determined upfront and there is rarely ever room for the expenses to get larger, only smaller.

Once the offer is written, it will be negotiated with the promoter, agents, and managers of the talent.

Tying Up Loose Ends:

As a promoter, tasks will include securing sound, sound engineer, crew, marketing, tickets, scheduling, sponsors, permits and dealing with different unique issues as they arise.

It will be important to monitor certain things the day of the show such as security, box office, stage-managing, load-in, load-out, and the settlement at the end of the show.

Being diligent and ensuring that your event is successful from a production and financial standpoint will distinguish you from other professionals in the same field. Success in the music industry relies heavily on reputation. Once people see that you're able to manage all aspects of planning and executing a successful event, the more events you'll be contracted to do.

Renting A Venue:

If you are renting a venue for a live show, it is very important to be diligent in making sure that nothing is overlooked. Be sure to get whatever permits you need, check city noise ordinances, obtain a license for food and drink, get the required police detail (will vary based upon the size of your event), know whether or not you will need to inform the fire marshal of the event. Always err on the side of overstaffing your event.

Be careful when budgeting your event. Plan for things to cost more than you anticipate.

The Show

First and foremost, it is important to understand that your career hinges on your reputation for how you treat the people that you work with, as well as how you treat the fans of the musicians. Be sure to take the time to establish a strong rapport with everyone you encounter in order to make every show a positive experience for everyone. Before leaving the venue, personally thank the soundman, the bartenders, the wait staff, and the bookers of the show. Being personable goes a long way in the music business.

End the show, load up your equipment and leave the venue in a timely manner. The staff is trying to go home. They have likely already been at the venue for a very long time. If you know that you will want to hang out extensively after a show, plan for an after-party at a nearby establishment.

Reflection

It is important to evaluate every performance in order to understand what works well during your live performance and what can use improvement. When evaluating your performance, critique your technical performance (how well you performed the songs), your stage presence, your set list, and the fan interaction. You should consider audience reaction. Make note of the great moments in the show. What exactly made those moments great! Was it lighting, special sound effects, heartfelt patter…what? How can you consistently reproduce those moments in every performance?

Chapter 2

PHYSICAL MERCHANDISE

Merchandising is one of the best ways to ensure that you will make a profit. Not only can merchandise put money directly in your pocket when it is sold, but merchandise can also double as advertisement. If a fan buys a t-shirt from you, they will most likely wear it, which will help to promote your brand. Of all merchandise, items such as t-shirts, hoodies, and things that you can wear sell better than any other items. Clothing items often sell better than CD's. Fans are happy to publically represent your music. The best way to sell a lot of merchandise is to perform live.

Having physical merchandise such as shirts, sweatshirts, hats, and stickers at your show can greatly increase your profit each night that you perform live. Fans are much more likely to buy your merchandise while they are still excited and caught up in the moment at your concert. Be sure that you have someone designated to be at your merch table the whole night and that you accept credit cards. You can order credit card readers for free from websites such as squareup.com or Paypal.com. The company will just take a small percentage from each sale. In large indoor venues, it is sometimes difficult to get a consistent cellular Internet connection (on your phone or Ipad). Be sure to ask for the venue's wifi login info so that you can log onto their wifi if you're having trouble getting a cellular connection on your device. It would be awful to miss out on sales because of avoidable technical difficulties.

It's also important to assure that you have an adequate amount of smaller currency to make change when customers pay in cash. A customer may give you a $50 bill for a $15 purchase. You'll want to be prepared. Depending upon the pricing of your merchandise, you'll want to have an abundance of $10 bills, $5 bills and singles available. You'll also want to have coins available.

It is customary for most venues to take a percentage of merchandise sales. A common arrangement is that the venue will take 30 percent of the merchandise sales, which leaves 70 percent for the band.

When choosing what merchandise to manufacture, be sure to look at your specific demographic. Across the board, the large majority of musical acts will want to print t-shirts, which for most acts represents about 80% of the total merchandise sold. However, you want to also get creative with your merchandise and sell what fans will buy.

I had the privilege of touring with music icon Wiz Khalifa. He has been very creative with his branding and his merchandise. He has secured himself in the marketplace and he plays to his niche. Wiz is an open supporter of marijuana. He came out with a new line of his own personal rolling papers for marijuana use. Wiz recognized his demographic, and made a product that his fan base would be happy to support. He still has t-shirts and other more traditional merchandise, but for this specific product, he looked at what he could provide to his fans that was unique.

Be sure that you do not skimp on the design of your merchandise. Take the time necessary to plan out what you want to release. After all, if it doesn't look cool, no one will buy it. When it comes to t-shirts, sometimes simple is better. Also, your designs will have to undergo silkscreen printing. Silkscreen printing does not translate to garments like it does to paper. The more simple and iconic the design, the easier it will translate to a t-shirt or hat. Furthermore, through my experience, I have seen that more simple designs appeal to a larger and more varied audience base. Maximize your potential for merchandise sales by offering a design that will appeal to the largest audience possible.

When deciding on colors for your merchandise, you want to remember that the more colors you choose, the more the shirt will cost to print. During the printing process, the printer will need to make a screen for every color you choose. Therefore, the more colors, the more screens, the more money you will spend. Another way that costs can quickly mount up is based upon where you want your designs on the t-shirt itself. Printing on the sleeves and back might look really cool, but for every location you add on the shirt, the more you will pay. Look at your budget and analyze if it is worth it to add extra colors and extra printing locations on the shirt. Will adding these extra dynamics to the shirt make it that much more appealing to fans?

Once merch is printed, the goal is to sell as much as possible. How you do this? Here are some tips:

1. While you're on stage, mention that you have a merch table at the show. If people aren't aware that you have merch for sale, they can's possibly purchase it. Do not be ashamed to call attention to your merchandise.

2. Be sure that your merchandise table is located in a highly trafficked area of the venue. Generally, you will find good locations near the entrance or exit of the venue. Every venue is different. Analyze where your table will be in front of the most eyes.

3. Keep your prices reasonable and make your prices visible.

4. Make sure that you have someone running your merchandise table that is a good sales person. Work out a commission system with them where the amount they earn is directly correlative to how much they sell. This way, they will have an incentive to sell more.

5. Offer bundles to fans. For example, if you sell a CD for $10 and a t-shirt for $15, advertise that you will sell them together for $20. (A $5 dollar savings)

6. Offer something small for free with each purchase. You can offer stickers, posters, etc.

7. ACCEPT CREDIT CARDS. This is very easy nowadays. You can get credit card processing tools for free or for very cheap from companies like Square Up (www.squareup.com).

8. Play out frequently. The more shows you play, the more opportunity you will have to sell merchandise.

9. Have the crew wear your merchandise.

10. Have the merchandise salespeople wear your merchandise.

11. Leave some t-shirts behind at the venue for some of the venue staff to wear. This will keep you in the minds of the staff so that you can more easily book subsequent shows.

12. Don't be afraid to give merchandise away. Again, as I said earlier, merchandise is not only a product that returns an immediate profit, but it is also advertisement.

Just like selling anything else, presentation is everything. Think about what your experience is like when you go into your favorite clothing store at the mall. Try to recreate that at your merchandise table. When heading to the venue to sell merchandise, make sure you bring with you the following things to make your table more presentable and appealing to your fans:

- A banner with the artist name
- Portable lights (to light up your product)
- A cash box
- Clips for hanging t-shirts/hoodies
- Tape
- Markers and pens
- Display shelves for CD's

- A sign to display prices
- Mailing list signups
- Scissors
- Table cloth (Most tables that venues will give you for merchandise are not pretty. You will want to cover them with a nice looking cloth).

If you want to run your band like a business, you will need to calculate things like ROI (return on investment), profit margin, turnover (how quickly your product sells), and keep track of your inventory.

- Return On Investment (ROI): This is how much you would make if you sold all of your merchandise order subtracted by the total cost of ordering the merchandise. For example, if it costs $500 to order a box of 100 t-shirts, and you sell all of those shirts for $20. Your return on investment would be $1500.

- Profit Margin: This is the percentage of how much you make per item. If a shirt costs $5 to make and you sell it for $20, you have a profit margin of 75%. Different kinds of products will have different margins. The reason the profit margin is important to analyze because it tells you how profitable each item is. A good margin is between 40%-60%.

- Turnover: This is an indicator of how fast your merchandise sells. If you order 100 shirts at a time and you sell 500 in a year, you would have a turnover of 5. You want to have a high turnover.

- Inventory: You want to always keep track of how much merchandise you have. You should count merch before and after every show in order to keep track. You also want to have accurate counts of each size and color of your merchandise.

Aside from selling merchandise at live performance, it will also be advantageous to set up an online merchandise store so that your products are readily accessible to your fans at all times. Websites like bigcartel.com specialize in providing suitable platforms for musicians to sell their merchandise.

Chapter 3

DIGITAL MERCHANDISE

The Internet has turned into an incredible way to garner new fans, and reinforce the relationship that you have with your current fans. By launching successful social media campaigns, you can build up to the release of various digital merchandise products.

Recently I have seen many musicians selling digital items that are very appealing to fans. These items include music, PDFs, videos, lyric books, live concerts, and other things that can be experienced online. These products encourage interaction with fans and allow musicians more opportunity to produce consumable content to release. One thing that is great about digital merchandise is that it often costs little or nothing to release a product. Unlike physical merchandise, which you have to buy and have inventory of, digital merchandise does not have to be kept on hand.

Brainstorm what you can bring to fans online that you might not be able to provide them in person. Remember that the Internet allows fans a more intimate view into the lives of their favorite musicians. You can play to this advantage of the Internet. For example, fans love seeing behind the scenes footage of their favorite artists. My advice to every artist is to film a documentary. Documentaries go behind the scenes and give insight into the lives of the band members. Advertise the documentary on social media and once the documentary is finished, put it online and charge the fans to watch it.

Don't be afraid to seek sponsors for the digital merchandise that you put online. If you are going to be selling a live concert online, contact companies that you may have a relationship with to see if they would pay you to put their logo in the credits or somewhere in the video. For further information on sponsorships, read the "SPONSORSHIPS" chapter.

Many people in the music industry have complained that the Internet has ruined music because of illegal downloading and streaming services that do not pay artists fairly, but these people are overlooking the doors that have been opened as a result of this incredible medium to communicate with fans. When using the Internet, be innovative. Take the time to map out how you would like to approach your Internet presence, and use it as a tool to increase profit and raise awareness of your music.

The challenge in digital merchandise is in the marketing. A strong social media presence is imperative. You need to have the reach and power to be able to drive fans to your products. Instead of posting a lot of digital content and hoping fans will find it, put most of your efforts into building your social media channels and building an Internet relationship with your fans.

Chapter 4

CD SALES

The Major Label Model

The price of the average CD has gone down drastically in the new millennium as a result of the ease in which fans can get their favorite artists music for free. In order to attempt to combat fans from file sharing, CD's have been made more affordable. The truth of the matter is that unless you are selling millions of albums, many major label artists do not make much money from CD sales anymore.

In the making of a CD, here are the key players and the percentage of sales that they get. Different albums have different breakdowns for percentages but this is an average approximation:

Artist (6.3%)
Producer (2.2%)
Songwriters (4.5%)
Distributor (22%)
Manufacturing (5%)
Retailer (30%)
Record label (30%)

If your CD is for sale in stores for $16.00 and you are a band of four that writes your own material, you will receive a royalty rate of 11%, however your producer will earn 3% of that, which will leave you at a net royalty of 8%. Therefore, $16.00 - $8.32 (30% for retailers, 22% for distributors) = $7.68.[2]

Now let's round $7.68 up to $8.00 just to make the numbers easier to work with. $8.00 - $2.00 (25% for packaging deducted by the label) = $6.00 x 8% - $0.48/ Therefore, the artist would make $0.50 per CD sold.[2]

So let's say the artist sells $500,000 copies. According to the above breakdown, the artist would receive $250,000. However, many times the record label will deduct another 15% for promotional and review copies for radio and magazines. Therefore, $250,000 - $ 37,500 (15% for promo copies) = $212,500. Also, the record label still has to make their royalties, which is another 30%. So now you have to calculate $212,500 - $63,750 (30% for record label royalties) = $148,750.[2]

Now we have to factor in all of the costs we accumulated to make the album. Some of these costs are the engineer, equipment rental, studio costs, etc… For the sake of this hypothetical, we will say those costs accumulate to $85,000. So with these costs taken out, we are now at $63,750.[2]

In many cases there is more than one person in the band. Let's say there are 4 people in the band. This leaves $15,937.50 per person in the band.[2]

As demonstrated in this hypothetical situation, there are a lot of expenses that go into making a CD in a major label situation and the profit for musicians is not nearly as fruitful as it used to be.[2]

The Do-It-Yourself Model

It is now easier than ever to self release an album both digitally and physically.

Digitally, there are great companies like Tunecore and CD Baby that will release your album to iTunes, Amazon, Spotify and many other music stores and streaming services. They will also give you as much as 90% of the profit from your sales.[1] The upside is that this is a quick and easy way to get your music out for sale and on streaming platforms. Also, you do not have to worry about investing a lot of money into the inventory of having a bunch of physical CD's laying around that may never get sold. The downside to releasing music this way as opposed to a major label is that you do not have the promotional backing for getting your product in front of as many eyes as possible.

As we discussed in the merchandise chapter, having physical products for sale at your concerts is much more appealing to fans than telling them to go home after a show and purchase a CD online. It is certainly beneficial to invest in physical CD's because it increases the value of the product for many consumers. Instead of purchasing a file of a CD off of iTunes, many fans would like to spend the same amount of money on a tangible CD.

Chapter 5

VINYL SALES

Vinyl suffered a severe decline at the end of the 1980's when the cassette came into the mix. Once the CD became the main way for music to be sold, the vinyl became obsolete. In the new millennium, all physical music sales have suffered because of distribution mediums like iTunes that distribute digitally.

Strangely, vinyl records have experienced resurgence. CD sales have declined 32.5% while vinyl sales have increased 52.1% over the last year. Vinyl records amassed $226 million dollars during the first half of 2015 alone.[3]

Companies like Urban Outfitters have helped to bring the vinyl album back to the spotlight. Many artists are releasing vinyl albums as limited edition items for their fans. Vinyl offers fans a ritual experience that they value where they can interact with and handle something physical.

Vinyl records will never be able to compete with other more mainstream forms of distribution, but vinyl records do serve as a great niche market that fans can really latch onto. As a musician, it may behoove you to order a small number of vinyl recordings and have them be a limited edition product that fans want to have to show loyalty to your brand.

Chapter 6

DIGITAL MUSIC SALES

Digital downloading is a huge method of distributing music. It takes away the hassle of heading to the record store, and allows the consumer to download music straight to their device of choice. Although illegal downloading has taken a big chunk out of music sales in general, digital music sales are crucial to making a profit with your music. There are services such as iTunes, eMusic, Spotify, Amazon, and Rhapsody that have created an opportunity for major and independent labels to sell music to a large and diverse market. Additionally, with selling music digitally, there is little overhead costs.

Now before I start explaining how great selling your music digitally is, let's not completely abandon the traditional method of CD printing. There is still a market for physical CD's and studies show that 66% of people still prefer them. Selling physical CD's at shows can be much more advantageous than waiting and hoping that your fans will go home after your show and purchase your music.[4]

As an independent artist, you will need to make sure to get your CD up to commercial standards before releasing it digitally. It is imperative that your product sounds its best. In addition to ensuring that the music quality is excellent, you will also need to have album artwork to submit, along with the track credits. Don't rush through the album artwork aspect of your release. Remember that your artwork is the first thing that the consumer will see when contemplating whether they will purchase your music or not. You want your album artwork to be enticing.

Before selling your music on any online store, you will need a UPC code for your release. A UPC code is basically a barcode that will track your release. Generally, you can go through your CD duplication company for this code. For no more than $50, you will be assigned a UPC code for your release.[5] You will be able to use this code on both a physical CD and your digital distribution. Another option for getting a UPC code, is to use "CD Baby" (www.cdbaby.com). They are an online store and a major player in the digital distribution market. They will assign you a UPC for $20. There are also other websites that can assign you a code, just simply google "UPC Code". Overall, I recommend using CD Baby.[5]

Next you will need to find a distributor. Unless you are a major artist, you will most likely not have the clout to deal directly with the major platforms from which you would be releasing your music. Therefore, you will need an established distributor to aid in the process. When finding a distributor, you will want to make sure that you will continue to own all rights to your own music, and that the relationship is a non-exclusive licensing agreement. If you are confused or don't understand anything during the process, contact an experienced entertainment lawyer. In the event that you do choose an agreement where you will be signing away the ownership rights to your material, make sure that the pay cut is fair. The average payout is about 60 cents per song download, and most digital distribution services will take about a 10% cut of that. There are two leading digital distribution services. Those services are CD Baby and Tunecore.[5]

CD Baby is partnered with iTunes, and many of the other digital platforms. They also not only set your CD up to be sold digitally, but if you would like to sell real copies, they will sell from their online store. They can handle all of the digital encoding of your material for you so that it is of the highest quality.

Tunecore is similar to CD Baby, however they only do digital distribution. Tunecore is also partnered with iTunes and will release your music to many other digital platforms. They do not make any claim to your material and will offer you a free UPC code. I have used Tunecore extensively in the past and they are great.

Digital sales are crucial to maximizing your profit as a musician because of the ease in which consumers can go online and purchase your material. Do not overlook this revenue stream and be sure to promote your digital offerings. For example, if you release music via iTunes, put the iTunes logo on your social media pictures and your promotional pieces. This will let your fans know that your music is available for purchase.

Chapter 7

STREAMING

Streaming music means to listen to music in "real time" instead of downloading a file to your computer and listening to it later. Royalties are generated when your songs are streamed on on-demand services such as Rhapsody and Spotify. Your publisher will receive your royalty payments from Harry Fox or another mechanical licensing agent. The publisher then pays the songwriter/composer of the song.

Music streaming has become a fairly controversial topic within the music industry recently. Because of the minimal amount that music-streaming services pay, artists such as Taylor Swift and Adele have opted not to release some of their music to streaming services in order to drive fans to purchase their music. This has served them well and has resulted in their albums placing very high on the charts. Taylor Swift was able to sell over one million album copies in the first week of her release, which can be attributed to her opting not to make her album available for streaming. However, most artists do not have this kind of leverage.

While streaming services may not compensate musicians handsomely, they make the artist's music accessible to fans who then will hopefully buy merchandise or purchase a concert ticket.

The industry is changing rapidly, and instead of fighting the change by clinging onto old revenue models, we need to adjust and adapt to what is happening around us in the industry. Music streaming is very popular among a large portion of music fans.

How do musicians make money from music streaming, you ask? I investigated Spotify, a leading music streaming service, and have included some figures.

In January of 2014, an artist receiving 10,000 streams in Spotify and controlling the rights to their recording and composition made $90.64. In December 2014, an artist with the same number of streams and ownership made $74.72, which is a decrease of -17.56%. The amount earned by the songwriter/publisher as a Mechanical Royalty each time a recording of their song was streamed in 2014 went down -5.37% from $0.00071961 in January to $0.000681 in December. The amount earned for a sound recording each time it was streamed in 2014 went down -17.39% from $0.0074199 in January to $0.0061296 in December.

The reason that streaming profits are decreasing is because monthly per-stream rates are calculated by dividing the money in the royalty pot (Spotify Reported Gross Revenue) by the number of streams in that month. The decrease in the per-stream rate is occurring due to the number of streams per month growing at a more rapid rate than the revenue.[6]

While streaming may not be the most lucrative way to make money for most musicians, I still strongly recommend that you put your music on streaming platforms. Regardless of your genre of music, a lot of your target demographic will most likely be on these streaming sites and you will most likely want to make your music readily available to them.

Chapter 8

SONGWRITING

Not all musicians compose music that they will themselves perform. A very viable way of earning an income is to write songs for other musicians, or to compose music specifically for film and television. Like many other revenue streams, your success very much correlates to how talented you are at your craft, however there are ways to greatly increase your success with songwriting.

First and foremost, even though songwriting is a very artistic endeavor, it is important to treat this endeavor as a business. I recommend that every songwriter do at least one "business" thing every day. This means networking, making phone calls, sending emails, following up on songs that you have previously submitted, working on your website, etc. By making a rule that you will do at least one business thing every day, you will have done 365 things during the course of a year that can help your songwriting career.

There are also songwriting groups that you can join. Songwriting groups can help to hold you accountable to your songwriting and allow you to be around others that are just as committed to songwriting. This is a great way to build a network of other songwriters that have similar goals as you. If you are not able to find a local songwriting group in your area, try to contact other songwriters that you know of to create one. By meeting every week, you will develop your songwriting skills.

Publishers are incredibly helpful for songwriters, however they are not necessary in order to have initial success in songwriting. Work every day to build your catalog of songs. When it comes time to get a publisher, they will be much more likely to work with you if you have a deep catalog of material instead of just a couple of songs. Furthermore, if you can get to the level where you are able to write and broker your material on your own, you may not need a publisher at all. Not having a publisher puts more money in your pocket.

While you are compiling your catalog of quality music, it is important to pitch the songs. In order to pitch them, you must first research outlets for your music. There are organizations that can help put songwriters together with industry professionals looking for songs. Also, be sure to network at every possible opportunity. Most industry professionals will be more prone to do business with someone that they personally know, instead of someone that has contacted them online. If you are able to pitch one song per week, you will have pitched 52 songs in an entire year, which will greatly increase your odds of getting a placement.

Reply promptly to every person that contacts you regarding your music. You never know what opportunities can come from these communications. Make yourself accessible to anyone that takes an interest in your work.

Chapter 9

LICENSING

Music licensing is constantly around us. When you hear music on the radio, it is licensed. When you hear music on the television, it is licensed. When you hear music in a restaurant, it is licensed. Music licensing can take several different forms.

The need for music licensing arises out of copyright law that is intended to protect the intellectual property of artists:

The copyright code of the United States (title 17 of the U.S. Code) provides for copyright protection in sound recordings. Sound recordings are defined in the law as "works that result from the fixation of a series of musical, spoken, or other sounds, but not including the sounds accompanying a motion picture or other audiovisual work." Common examples include recordings of music, drama, or lectures. Copyright in a sound recording protects the particular series of sounds "fixed" (embodied in a recording) against unauthorized reproduction and revision, unauthorized distribution of phonorecords containing those sounds, and certain unauthorized performances by means of a digital audio transmission. The Digital Performance Right in

Sound Recordings Act of 1995, P.L. 104-39, effective February 1, 1996, created a new limited performance right for certain digital transmissions of sound recordings.

Several things can be copyrighted in a sound recording for a song.

- The actual sounds itself – the performance of the work.
- The notes that the musicians play to create the song – they could be embodied in sheet music.
- The lyrics for the song – they can be written down on a sheet of paper.

Once a composition has been made, the person who created the composition owns the song and has the copyright. Technically, the registration process with the copyright office is not officially necessary in order for a creator of a piece to own a copyright. The creator of a composition is the rightful owner at the time the song is made; however to enforce a copyright in court, registration is required.

Whoever owns the copyright then has the option to sell the rights to the song, and also prevent anyone else from using the music, the lyrics or performance of the song. The song can be licensed any way that the owner chooses.

Licensing the Song

In the case of most popular songs, there are several different parties involved with the song:

- The label owns the actual sound recording – the performance of the song as recorded in the label's studio.

- The publisher works on behalf of the song's composer (the person who wrote/arranged the music) and the songwriter (the person who wrote the lyrics). The composer and songwriter probably own the actual copyrights for the song, and the publisher represents them in all business dealings.

If a party wants to use a song for any reason, they must obtain rights from the publisher and possibly from the label as well (if you are planning to use a specific recorded performance). Here are some examples of when you would need to obtain rights:

- [ ] You own a radio station and you want to play a song on your station.

- [ ] You own a restaurant and you want to play songs as background music.

- [ ] You are making a commercial and you want to use a song in the commercial.

- [ ] You are making a toy and you want it to play a song when a child pushes a button.

- [ ] You are making a video production and you want a song as background music.

It has been estimated that half a billion dollars trade hands every year through licensing fees.

ASCAP and BMI

If you own a radio station or a restaurant and you want to broadcast or play music, you will need to obtain public performance rights – the right to play music that the general public will hear in one way or another. If you own a radio station playing hundreds of songs per day, it would be a daunting task to obtain performance rights from every publisher. For this reason, public performance rights licensing is handled by two companies. They are ASCAP (American Society of Composers Authors and Publishers) and BMI (Broadcast Music Incorporated). Each of these companies handles about 4 million songs each.[7]

A radio station will usually purchase a "blanket license" from ASCAP and BMI in order to be able to broadcast music. The "blanket license" allows the radio station to play anything it would like throughout the year. ASCAP and BMI then decide how to divide up the money among the rightful owners.

Any establishment that wants to play music that will be heard by the general public needs a license as well. There is a form that establishments fill out that will then determine the exact license they need.

If a license is not purchased and you get caught, you can be sued. The fines can be thousands of dollars.

Commercials and Film

If an individual would like to use a song in a TV or radio commercial, they will need a Master Use License from the label and a Synchronization License (TV) and/or a Transcription License (Radio) from the publisher. The fees for synchronization licenses vary greatly with the usage and importance of the song.

Here are some examples for typical prices for these types of licenses:

☐ Low End TV Usage (example: music is playing from a jukebox in a scene, but no one in the scene is paying attention to the music) -- Free to $2000 for a 5-year license. In a film, the fee would be $10,000 in perpetuity.

☐ A more popular song is worth more. Around $3,000 for TV and $25,000 for film.

☐ A song used for the theme song for a film could get $50,000 to $75,000.

☐ Commercials often times get a lot more money. A song can get anywhere from $25,000 to $500,000 plus per year. The typical range for a well-known song is $75,000 to $200,000 for a one-year national usage in the United States, on television and radio.[7]

Happy Birthday to You!!!

One of the most common music licensing stories surrounds the song "Happy Birthday to You." The song was written in 1893 by Mildred and Patty Hill and first published with the words "good morning to you." The words "Happy Birthday to You" were first seen in print in 1924, although the author is unknown. The copyright was registered in 1934 in a court case involving a musical called "As Thousands Cheer" by Irving Berlin. The Clayton F. Summy Company became the son's publisher in 1935. Through a series of purchases and acquisitions, the song now belongs to AOL Time Warner. ASCAP represents the song for public performance licensing.[8]

The copyright to "Happy Birthday to You" should have expired in 1991, but the Copyright Act of 1976 extended it, and the Copyright Term Extension Act of 1998 extended it again, so the song is at least protected until 2030.[8]

"Happy Birthday to You" brings in about $2 million per year in licensing fees. Whenever you hear the song in a movie, TV shows or commercial, a licensing fee has been paid.[8]

Samples

Licensing is also required when samples of other songs are used. Even if just a few notes are being used, a license must be obtained. Otherwise the individual using the sample will end up paying penalty fees when the song is played in public.

Hip-Hop: Beats

I have worked quite a bit with hip-hop artists that work with producers in order to get "beats" or tracks that they can then sing and rap over. A beat generally contains a drum loop pattern with some other synthetic sounds over it.

There are two general types of licenses, non-exclusive and exclusive.

A *non-exclusive license* gives the rights to the artist to use the master recording beat to create a song with the artist lyrics, raps, chorus, etc... However, the producer or whoever wrote the song still retains copyright ownership of the beat. The copyright holder also has the right to license the beat to whomever he wants to until the beat is purchased exclusively.

Through the artist recording their own lyrics on the beat, they have now created a derivative work of the song. What this means is that the artist owns a copyright of the work that they created on the beat that they licensed but there is no copyright claim to the original music contained in the beat.

Usually *non-exclusive licenses* have limits on how many units you can sell. If the artist is optimistic about the amount of copies they can sell, they may want to look into obtaining an exclusive license.

An exclusive license gives the artist complete control over what is done with the master recording. The artist can add as many derivate recordings as they wish and they have unlimited rights to sell as many copies as they wish. Some producers differ on how they define exclusive... Just because you have exclusive rights to the master doesn't give you exclusivity to the composition. The license could just be for audio recording and the producers or original writers may not be ok with you licensing the original beat that the artist purchased to a TV show for example. Also, licensors will sometimes not let you re-sell or license the master to another entity, such as a record company or another producer. Most producers will also want credit for their work.

Chapter 10

PUBLISHING ROYALTIES

Songwriters actually make money through publishing royalties. A large publishing revenue that you will earn as a songwriter is a performance royalty, which will be covered later in the book, but a larger revenue stream is the mechanical royalty. Mechanical royalties cover any copyrighted audio composition that is rendered mechanically. Basically, every time a song you have written is manufactured to be sold in a CD, downloaded on a digital music retail site, or streamed through services like Spotify, you are owed a mechanical royalty.

In the United States, the statutory royalty rate is generally equal to 9.1 cents per reproduced copy of the song, regardless of whether or not those songs are sold. For example, if someone covers one of your songs and they manufacture 1000 CD's, they owe you $91, regardless of whether the CD's were ever actually purchased by customers.[10]

Additionally, you are also owed a mechanical royalty for the sales of your music on your own albums. If you are acting as your own label and putting out music that you have written, you will effectively be paying that royalty to yourself from album proceeds.

In the United States, retailers like iTunes and Amazon will pass on your mechanical royalty as part of the net payment for the sale of the MP3. However, in many countries outside the United States, mechanical royalties are set aside by the retailer, and then paid to collection societies who then distribute the royalties to publishers and writers. In order to collect these international mechanical royalties, you will need to register your music with many royalty collection societies around the world. You can utilize services like CD Baby who will register your songs directly with societies around the world and will ensure that you get nearly all the publishing royalties you are owed.

Chapter 11

DIGITAL ROYALTIES

Digital royalties are fees that digital radio services, such as Pandara, SiriusXM, webcasters and cable TV music channels are required by law to pay for streaming music. There are companies like Sound Exchange that take these payments, allocate the fees to the recordings according to how often each song was played, and then pay the featured artists and copyright owners of those recordings.

By law, 45 percent of performance royalties are paid directly to the featured artist on the recording, 5 percent are paid to a fund for non-featured artists (session musicians and background singers), and the other 50 percent of the performance royalties are paid to the owner of the sound recording (whoever owns the master), which can be a record label or an artist who owns their masters.[10]

In the event that your digital performance royalties go unclaimed, after three years your royalties get distributed to major labels and popular artists based on market share. Therefore, if you don't register to receive your royalties, you will lose them!

Chapter 12

LIVE PERFORMANCE ROYALTIES

Live performance royalties refer to the royalties paid to the songwriter when one of their songs is played live. However, a live performance of a song doesn't always means it actually has to be played "live", like in a concert setting. A live performance of a song can also refer to a public airing of a recorded version of a song, such as radio play, television play, etc. A general rule is that any time a song is played publicly, the songwriter is owed a live performance royalty.

Tracking these performances is a lot to manage. Therefore, instead of musicians and publishers taking on the task of tracking down money owed to them from live performances, they turn to performance rights organizations (or PRO's). In the United States, the performance rights organizations are comprised of Broadcast Music, Incorporated (BMI), American Society of Composers, Authors and Publishers (ASCAP), and the Society of European Stage Authors and Composers (SESAC). The performance rights organizations issue licenses to anyone who uses live music. The organizations then collect licensing fees and royalties to then distribute payments to the members of the organizations.

As a musician, you will want to apply for a membership with one of the societies. Publishers many times have relationships with all of the societies in order to collect payments for all of their songwriters.

When a publisher and songwriter join a PRO, each is awarded 50% of each of the songs they register. Therefore, when royalties are collected, the PRO will pay each of them half. The organization will pay the publisher and the songwriter directly. This way, each party is paid at the same time, and the songwriter will not have to wait to be paid their share from the publishing company.

Performance rights organizations issue blanket licenses to companies who play live music. A blanket license gives the company the right to use all of the songs in the catalog of that performance rights organization. For example, if a radio station secures a blanket license with ASCAP, they are then allowed to play any song that is included in the ASCAP catalog. The licensing fee for each company depends on a number of factors. For example, the fee might be contingent on the size of the business, how often music is played, the size of their audience, the manner in which the music is played, etc. Some businesses might get away with paying a small fee whereas others might have to pay millions.

I'm sure you are wondering how all of these royalties are kept tracked. The truth is, it is nearly impossible. Each organization uses different methods to track what royalties are owed. Tracking generally involves a mix of digital tracking along with reporting by the license holder. The data is then used to determine what percentage or share of royalties should be distributed to each member. Obviously, there are going to be plays that are not reported or potentially even over reported, however the PRO's main mission is to make the best educated guess supported by data. Digital plays are nearly always 100% paid out on, because digital groups are able to deliver 100% complete playlists to the PRO's.

Performance Rights Groups

Broadcast Music Incorporated is arguably the largest performance rights organization in the world. They have a catalog of 8.5 million songs, and are made up of over 650,000 songwriters, composers and music publishers. BMI collects royalties in the United States and is the leading choice for non-US acts looking to collect their songwriting royalties in the US. This organization is free to join for songwriters, and $150 to join as a publisher. You do not need a publishing company to collect your publisher's share of royalties from BMI.[11]

The American Society of Composers, Authors and Publishers is another major royalty collection group based in the United States. ASCAP has 500,000 songwriters, composers and music publishers. ASCAP is $50 for songwriters to join and $50 for publishers. In order to collect your publishers share of royalties as an ASCAP member, you need to have an ASCAP publishing company.[11]

The Society of European Stage Authors and Composers is the only PRO in the United States that is not open to all songwriters. You must receive an invitation to join. SESAC represents over 400,000 songs on behalf of its 30,000 members. According to the SESAC website, "SESAC is the fastest growing and most technologically adept of the nation's performing rights companies." There is no fee associated with joining this society, however, as mentioned above, you must be invited to join.[11]

Chapter 13

SESSION WORK/FEATURES

Session work can be difficult to find because it is comprised of an under the radar, secret society of musicians. One of the hardest parts of working as a session musician can be to find your first few jobs.

Success in the music industry in general is often dependent upon who you know. You will want to look into any other musicians that you know will be recording soon, or call up any friends who might work in a recording studio. Even if you don't know anyone that can give you work right away, you will still want to make these connections and let people know that you are looking for session work. The more people in the industry that know you are looking for session work, the higher becomes your chance of getting called.

Studios often get asked where they find certain players. You will want to be sure to be on their radar. The competition can be very stiff in some cities but don't be discouraged. The hardest part of finding session work is getting into the circle of the other session musicians. Once you get in this circle, work will become easier to get. When talking to studios about your session work, make sure to mention your professionalism and experience with the recording process. Studio engineers would much rather work with a musician that knows how to record and will be easy to work with.

It can also be advantageous to let record labels know that you are a session musician. Many times they will need musicians for various recordings or they might even need someone to fill in for a show.

Similar to most other business, you want to make sure that you advertise your services everywhere you can. It will help you to post ads on craigslist, in local papers, flyers in record shops and studios, message boards, etc. To find session work, it is important to advertise to people who are working in the industry. Analyze where other musicians hang out and advertise there.

Work to separate yourself from the rest of the session musicians by offering unique services. If you can quickly learn an instrument or already know how to play a more obscure instrument, like a steel drum or glockenspiel, you will increase your marketability greatly. There are many session guitar and piano players, but some of these obscure instruments are more rare to find and can secure your niche in the marketplace.

In the event that the industry isn't paying attention to your services, you may want to consider making a small investment and booking a recording session for yourself. This way, you will be able to spend a few hours in the studio with the people that have a say in booking session work. Hopefully when they see you play, they will take a mental note and book you in the future. Additionally, this will render you a professional sample of your work that you can then use to vouch for your skill level and give yourself more credibility.

The music industry is one of the most competitive industries in which to find success. Always put yourself in situations where you'll meet fellow musicians and where people can hear you play. This kind of work is hard to get into, but once you are in the circle, you will get recurring calls for more work.

Features

Similar to session work, vocal artists can also do what is popularly referred to as "features" on another artists work. A "feature" is when an artist makes a guest appearance on another artists recording.

Features can be beneficial in two primary ways. First, the artist that is making the guest appearance will be compensated for their work. Features are ways for artists to make consistent money by having other artists pay them for their talents. Secondly, a feature will expose your name and talents to a larger audience once the recording is released.

I encourage artists to be selective with the feature work that they take on. While a feature might pay a nice sum of money upfront, it could potentially be damaging for your personal brand in the long run. Understanding your brand as a musician is important. Only work with songs that will fit your brand and that won't confuse your audience.

Chapter 14

SPONSORSHIPS

Many artists can use their "celebrity" status to their advantage through endorsements and sponsorships. They are in the public eye and the general public will often want to emulate the things that they do. There are many ways artists can benefit through sponsorships that include cash, extra promo materials, and gear.

The first thing you want to do when searching for a sponsorship collaboration is to identify your 'hit list" of local sponsors and start contacting them. It is important to analyze your personal brand as a musician in order to determine what kinds of products you can most easily advertise. For example, if you are an artist that is known for how stylishly you dress, it may be to your advantage to contact clothing companies that you like. They may be willing to pay you to wear their clothing for a photo shoot, for your next performance, or to post about them on social media.

You should aim to acquire as many sponsorship deals as possible. For example, each company may only pay you $200 per month to advertise their product, however if you can secure five of these deals, you can make a consistent $1000 per month for casually advertising products. You will want to seek sponsors who are not competitors with each other.

You wouldn't approach two clothing brands or two soft drink brands. You must give sponsors exclusivity in their market.

One of the most important aspects of securing a partnership deal is having a good pitch. You need to compile information that will show how the partnership will be beneficial to the sponsor.

Information to give to potential sponsors:

☐   Heading with band logo and the logo of the business you are pitching to at the top of the page

☐   Summary of what you are asking for (sponsorship for show, tour, festival, etc.)

☐   What you can do and plan to do for them

☐   Specified time period if there is one (annual contract? One show?). This can also be moved to the top heading as "An Annual Partnership Between…"

☐   What the business is to provide (signage, product, money)

The only reason that any company will enter a sponsorship agreement with you is if they feel as though they can benefit from it. Generally, they will want signage at a show, logo on flyers, logo on website, stage mentions, and mentions on social media pages. The more value you add to an agreement, the more money you can ask for.

When suggesting a partnership to a company, never overestimate your following. It is better to under-promise and over-deliver when it comes to anything in business.

Chapter 15

CROWDFUNDING

Crowdfunding has recently become an incredibly popular way for musicians to fund a project or venture by raising monetary contributions from a large number of people. This is generally done through websites like KickStarter, Indiegogo and Crowdfunder.

When brainstorming about your crowdfunding campaign, you will need to look internally and determine how much money you need, and what specifically you will do with the money. A lot of the appeal for fans to support your crowdfunding efforts is their desire to be a part of something big and important. They will want to know that their money will play a key role in accomplishing that goal. While determining how much money you need and what you will do with the money, put yourself in the fan's shoes and figure out what will make them want to be a part of your project.

Research the costs associated with your project and make sure nothing is overlooked. You want to make sure that the money that you are seeking from crowdfunders will be enough to cover all of your expenses. Be sure to get quotes from manufactures, insurers, lawyers, suppliers, distributers, and anyone else that will need to be a part of the process. Make a budget for your campaign and put all associated costs into the budget. This will also help the crowdfunders to see exactly what their money will be going towards.

An important part of the campaign is the presentation. Be sure to use videos and high quality photos for all of your promotional pieces for the campaign. Also, start to craft your story. Crowdfunders will be much more likely to donate to you if you have a story that goes along with the project you are embarking upon. For example, if you are trying to get your new CD funded, maybe make a short video about an experience that inspired your favorite song on the album. Or if your touring van broke down in Albuquerque, New Mexico, make a video about how great the tour was going and how you would appreciate the monetary support to keep the tour going.

Different platforms provide different specialties. Kickstarter is a great crowdfunding platform for musicians. Kickstarter generally focuses on creative ideas. It will be important to put your creative juices to work because of the high traffic of Kickstarter. The more creative and compelling your campaign is, the more likely that it will gain some attention and make it to their homepage. Indiegogo is another suitable option for musicians and they may be able to feature you more prominently on their homepage, newsletter, and social media outlets, however they don't have the same frequent traffic as Kickstarter.

Once you have your crowdfunding platform picked, you will then need to have a solid outline of your story, including "who, what, where, when, and why." Your explanation of the campaign should be clear, succinct, and to the point. Furthermore, your images and video should be in line with the theme of the campaign.

Crowdfunding campaigns offer the ability for the creator of the campaign to reward the crowdfunders. Generally, the rewards are granted based on the amount of money donated. Here is an example of some common rewards:

-Pledge $10 or more: Receive a signed CD
-Pledge $20 or more: Receive a signed CD and signed lyric sheet
-Pledge $30 or more: Get all of the above, and you will receive a CD with unrecorded songs recorded live
Pledge $50 or more: Receive all of the above, and you will receive a meet and greet at the next performance in your city
-Pledge $100 or more: Receive all of the above, and you will receive a personalized video posted to our social media pages thanking you for your contribution
-Pledge $200 or more: Receive all of the above, and you will receive a house concert (funder pays the costs of travel).

These are very basic examples. When thinking of rewards for your particular campaign, think about unique rewards that you could give your fans. Make sure that the rewards that you mention will be enticing to the fans and will make them want to donate. Also, the rewards don't necessarily have to cost you a lot to furnish. For many fans, it is worth it to them to donate even if it just means that they will get a chance to meet you at your next show.

Make sure to take into consideration any costs associated with getting the reward to the fans. As you may have noticed above, I included after the last reward that traveling costs would be at the funders expense. If the funder lived in Paris and you are located in Los Angeles, it could cost a pretty penny to fly to Paris when they only donated $200 in the first place. Be clear in letting the funder know if there will be any additional expenses for them to receive their reward.

Before launching your campaign, double-check your delivery date. Most campaigns do not deliver on time because the project takes longer than planned. Make sure that you will actually be able to deliver within the time that you are advertising.

It is beneficial to have a core team of people promoting the campaign with you. For musicians, you will want to get a street team of fans involved in spreading the word about your campaign. Have them share your videos and tell people about your project. You may even want to supply them with promotional materials that they can then use to promote more effectively. You will also want to pursue press to help reach more people. Draft a press release and contact the media to publicize your campaign.

Depending on the project, some organizations or business can provide networks of potential donors. Make a list of local organizations related to your project and ask if they would be willing to donate, or publicize your campaign through their social media and newsletters.

Have goals for different milestones during the campaign. Generally, 25% of the funding is raised within the first 24 hours. Keep track of this and try to determine if you are ahead of your goal, on track for your goal, or falling behind your goal. If you are working ahead of your goal, the crowdfunding sites themselves will be more likely to feature your project, which can help boost your earnings drastically.

Use all sorts of communication for your campaign. It is not enough to make the campaign page and hope money rolls in. You will need to be active on email, social media (twitter, facebook, instagram), blogs, media, personalized letters, etc. Make sure your fans are engaged and using all of these communication channels as well. Email can be more effective than many bands like to recognize. Don't be afraid to make an email list with family, friends, relatives, past teachers/coaches, or anyone else you know personally, in addition to fans. Many times the people that donate the most are the most unsuspecting. It could be a teacher that you had an 3rd grade that saw a lot of promise in you and wants to support your campaign. You never know.

Be sure to keep your funders updated with how the campaign is doing. After all, they are funding because they want to be a part of the project. Reward them with keeping them included.

When your campaign is over and you have reached your goal, thank everybody for being a part of your campaign and let them know what your future plans are.

Crowdfunding is a great way to not only raise money for your projects but it can also help immensely with your marketing tactics. If done according to these steps, you will be able to drive a large number of people to your crowdfunding page and hopefully people will know a lot more about your upcoming project.

Chapter 16

YOUTUBE

Youtube has become a popular platform for artists to not only release their content to a wide audience, but to also monetize from the content they post. Artists can post music videos, lyric videos, video blogs, and announcement videos, each one with the potential to go viral.

In order to get started, you will first need to set up your YouTube account. Each person's YouTube channel serves as their personal presence on YouTube. Creating a YouTube account will grant you access to other Google products like Gmail and Google Drive. Be sure to add keywords by navigating to the "Advanced" section of your Channel Settings. Your keywords should be relevant to your content. It is important to use a username that will be short, easy to remember, and will easily identify you to other people.

Once your channel is created, it is now time to add content. In the beginning, add high quality content that is not too long. Upload content regularly and be consistent with your uploads. By uploading regularly, you can help to hold an audience. People will be more likely to subscribe if you add content on a regular schedule, and maintain the schedule. When you post videos, be sure to tag your videos with key words that describe the content, as well as an eye-catching description. These will help drive people to your video from YouTube searches.

Once content is posted on a regular basis, it is time to focus on gaining an audience. Building the audience is a key component to increasing your monetization. You need people to watch your ads in order to make any money off of them. In order to get more of an audience, keep uploading content and try to get people hooked. Send your video out on Twitter and Facebook. Share it with people and distribute it everywhere you can on the Internet. Be sure to interact with your viewers by responding to comments and making occasional videos directly related to viewer comments and questions.

Finally, once you have gained an audience, efforts can now be placed on monetizing your videos. In order to start earning money from your videos, you will have to enable monetization, which means that you are allowing YouTube to place ads in your video. You will need to acknowledge that there is no copyrighted material in your video. You can monetize a video as it uploads by clicking the "Monetization" tab and checking the "Monetize with Ads" box. To monetize a video after it has been uploaded, open your "Video Manager" and click the "$" sign next to the video that you want to monetize. Click the "Monetize with Ads" box.

You can set up Google AdSense for free at the AdSense website. Click the "Sign Up Now" button to begin creating your account. You need either PayPal or a bank account and a valid mailing address as well as other information so AdSense can verify who you are and who to send the money to. You only gain money per ad click and a smaller amount per view but it adds up over time.

Once you have videos online that are monetized and being viewed, you can check out the analytics on them to see how they are performing. Click the "Analytics" option in your "Channel" menu. Here you can view estimated earnings, ad performance, video views, demographics and more. These tools can be used to see how your content is resonating with your audience. Through the analytics, you will better be able to identify what your fans like and don't like and can make adjustments accordingly for future videos.

Chapter 17

COVER GIGS

Often restaurants, coffee shops, bars, weddings, conferences and other events would prefer to book a cover band instead of a band that performs music that they have written. The reason for this is that people that want to hear music that they are familiar with. In most towns there will be businesses looking to hire entertainment for their guests, and a good cover band is the perfect choice to appeal to wide audiences. A good cover band will be able to connect with the audience and provide them with classics that they know and cherish. Getting gigs for your cover band can be difficult at first because you don't have a track record of previous gigs or referrals from satisfied customers, but with these five short steps, you will be able to get your cover band up and running.

1) First you will want to start a website. Creating a website for your band is the first initial step towards drawing business. If someone is searching for a cover band for their party, a visually appealing website will stand out to them and vouch for the credibility of your band. You will want to ensure that you have appropriate contact information, a compelling bio, recent pictures of the band, and a sample of your music. Once

you get a few gigs under your belt, your band will also want to add video from successful events that you have done.

2) The next step is to get your name out, and promote. When your website is built, you cannot simply rely on people to flock to it and begin to book you for events. You can try the conventional and effective method of printing and handing out posters, flyers and other advertising as a way to let people know about your band. Having printed ads will expose you to more potential clients. Additionally, business cards are very important for the viability of a cover band. You never know when you will meet your next client. If someone asks for your card, you will want to make sure that you are prepared with one. Keep your card simple and professional. It should at least contain your website, a name to contact, and a phone number.

3) Social media and website optimization should also be used in order to reach the largest number of people. If you frequently play cover gigs around the same city, post information about where your next gig will be to all of your social media channels. If people like your band and you play at a different bar around the city every Saturday night, those people just might make it a weekly event to see you at a different bar each weekend. Naturally, the more people that come to a bar to see you, the more money you can demand from each bar over time. Make information easy for people to find.

4) It will also behoove you to find a good manager. Ideally, the band's primary focus should be to make music. Therefore

delegating all business tasks to a qualified professional will help the band's success overall. It is important to choose a manager that you can trust since they will be responsible for your career and handling your money. Ask around and do your research to make sure that any manager you choose to work with is legitimate. Also make sure to have an agreement with them before working together. Refer to the artist manager chapter of this book to see further what you should have in an artist management contract. A legitimate manager will usually have a website that looks professional, will be easy to contact when needed, and won't take more money than they should. There should not be any suspicious fees required by a manager. Having a manager who knows and has connections at the nearby venues, and is nearby geographically will make the relationship a lot stronger and will result in more success with bookings.

5) Lastly, don't turn down too many opportunities. Many bands shoot themselves in the foot by being too arrogant. Without an established career, you're most likely not at the level yet where you are going to be booked at all of the venues that you would like. When starting out, it is important to work the gigs that you can and to build a solid reputation. The more gigs that you take starting out, the more you can network. Hopefully some of the people that are watching you perform can someday book you for their own event.

Preparation is key with this endeavor. By having your ducks in a row, you will be able to find opportunities and jump on them.

Chapter 18

MUSIC LESSONS/WORKSHOPS

Many musicians teach private lessons at some point in their careers. Sometimes musicians teach to supplement their income, and others teach as their main source of income. If you book enough students, teach at the right price, and exploit the internet, you can make pretty good money.

Building a clientele of students can take time. Private teachers have several different ways that they can run their business. Here are the various options:

Option 1: Teach through a school.

Option 2: Teaching in-home (at the students house) through a company.

Option 3: Teaching in-home (at the students house) on your own.

Option 4: Teaching through a music store (in store).

Option 5: Teaching at a private/home studio of your own.

Evaluate your current situation and determine which option will work best for you. If you want to minimize your responsibility of acquiring students, teaching through a school, with a company, or in a music store may be the best option for you. However, if you have the hustle to advertise your business, teaching on your own may be the best option because it allows for higher profit margins for each lesson.

In order to be successful in any business venture, you have to understand who your buyer is. For example, when teaching kids, it will not be a good idea you to angle your advertisements only to the child. You will also need to recognize who is paying for the lessons. You will need to sell your service to the parent and the child. Make sure the lessons are fun and that the child will want to see you every week.

In order to reach the parents, you will want to place ads in newspapers, distribute fliers in mailboxes, create brochures to hand out, contact the local school and speak to the music department for them to refer students to you. You'll want to contact music stores in your area and ask to be put on their private teacher list for music lessons, make business cards and have them ready to hand out, and write a letter that you can send to parents explaining what the lessons entail, price information, scheduling information, and contact information.

There are instruments that are more popular than others. If you want to maximize your clientele, it would be to your advantage to teach instruments such as piano, guitar, drums, and voice. Obviously, the more instruments you can teach well, the more customers you will appeal to.

Once you have acquired a substantial roster of students, consider throwing a recital. This will be a chance for students to showcase what they have learned during their time with you. Parents want to see their children engaged in productive activity and enjoying it. A recital is your chance to show the progress that the students have made and their love for the instrument that they have chosen. It will also give students the desire to strive in their lessons in anticipation of upcoming recitals.

Also, do not be afraid to use the Internet to teach music lessons. There are websites like takelessons.com where people can book private lessons. This can expand your reach of clients and allow you to teach all over the world. Instead of only having 70 people in your city interested in learning trombone, you could have 7,000 people right at your fingertips.

Workshops

I am a Consultant for a recording studio in Orlando, Florida that frequently holds workshops for musicians in the city. These workshops not only educate all in the room about the particular topic being taught, but they also provide a sense of community for everyone involved.

For one event we had a Producer Workshop. We had the best producers in the country come in and speak to a select group of 70 aspiring producers and students. We set up several stations where the attendees could learn about different aspects of producing and get a chance to ask questions of the experts.

Workshops can be a good way to educate, make a profit, but also promote your brand and your product. The 70 attendees that came to that event went on to tell their friends and family of the great time they had at the workshop. Because of the word of mouth press that we got from the attendees, we were able to throw several more events on the same topic.

You should run your workshop like an event and do so according to the steps for running an event that I outlined in the "Live Show" chapter.

Throwing Your Own Live Event

In addition to understanding the 18 revenue streams outlined in this book, it is also critical for anyone in the entertainment industry to understand how to effectively plan and execute an event. Planning an event can be daunting. It is important to have a clear-cut outline of the various tasks that will need to be completed in preparation for your event, whether it is a concert, cover gig, recital or workshop. This list will serve as a guide to make sure nothing is overlooked in the planning process.

Establish Goals and Objectives

☐   Before beginning to plan your event, it is important to establish the goals and objectives for the event. For example, if the goal is to throw a fundraiser that will raise a specified amount of money, you will be able to progress further in your planning with a clear idea of the goal. Establishing a general goal will to keep you on track.

Construct a Team and Delegate Tasks

☐ Delegating tasks effectively to team members will save you time and will allow you the ability to operate more effectively and efficiently. There should be a person in charge as an "Event Manager" or "Event Chair". After the person in charge has been established, split up others into the following subcommittees:

-Publicity
-Entertainment
-Speakers
-Venue Relations
-Sponsors
-Volunteer Management

Set A Date

☐ The next step is to pick a date that you can realistically hold the event. In order to properly sort out all logistics, you will want to begin to plan the event at least 3 months in advance. Make sure you are not planning the event on any religious holidays. Also, check with all parties involved (speakers, entertainment, etc…) to ensure that they are in fact available for the proposed date.

Brand The Event

☐   During this stage, you will establish the name of the event, establish a tagline, and create a logo. The name and tagline should serve as a succinct way of describing to the event-goer the event experience. The logo should also allude to the visuals that the event-goer will encounter when attending.

Lock In Your Plan

☐   Write out a plan for how the following activities will take place:

-Venue logistics, catering, contracts, permits, insurance, etc.

-Speakers: Getting confirmations from speakers and signing contracts.

-Entertainment: Getting confirmations from acts and signing contracts.

-Publicity and Promotion: Making signage, advertising on-line and off-line, printing flyers, printing brochures, posting to social media.

Administrative Process

☐   Determine how you will keep track of all different tasks such as registration, budget, guest lists.

Engage Sponsors

☐ By aligning with a sponsor, not only will you decrease the financial burden of throwing an event, but you will also have additional sources promoting your event. You can either ask sponsors to provide goods or services that will help the event to operate successfully, or they can offer money in exchange for promotion at the event.

Create A Publicity Plan

☐ Brainstorm on creative and effective ways of alerting your target market of the event. While social media is a great tool, it is also important to promote the event in a more direct way by personally reaching out to people. Hand out flyers, promote your event at other similar events, make a website for your event, etc.

Establish A Budget

☐ Reasonably predict how much each stage of your master plan will cost. Be sure to include a section of the budget for unexpected costs, as well as travel, food, etc.

Establish A Way To Measure Success

☐ When establishing a goal, it is also important to have a way to measure if the goal was reached or not. If the goal was to raise money, you will have a fairly easy way to measure the effectiveness. If the goal was to raise brand awareness, you can measure based on new social media followers.

FUNDING YOUR BUSINESS

Money is necessary to start your business in the most impactful way possible. When preparing to launch your music business, it will help to understand potential funding sources. In this segment, you will learn how investors work and how to communicate with them effectively.

Personal Funds

OK … first things first. It is imperative to have as much personal money invested in the startup as possible. The reason for this is that investors like seeing that the business owner(s) have "skin in the game." Give yourself enough time before going to investors to raise money. This shows that you have something to lose in the venture as well. It does not necessarily matter how much or little money you have invested in the business, what matters is that you have invested your own hard earned money and you do not want to lose it. By investing your own money first, you are showing the investor that you are serious about the venture and will take their money and input seriously.

Family and Friends

After you have put as much money as you can into the business, go to family and friends for additional funds. When investors see that family and friends haven't invested in your business, they become skeptical. An investor will wonder why your family and friends have not invested. They will think "if this persons family and friends, the people that know them best, haven't invested in this person, why should I?" Additionally, if family and friends have money invested, potential investors know that you will do your best to maintain the relationships that you have with those people and that you will be more likely to manage your business well to earn their money back. Convincing an investor to fund your project comes down to one factor; trust.

Crowd-Funding

Websites like Kickstarter, Indiegogo, and Rockethub encourage funders to donate money in exchange for benefits provided by the entity being funded. For example, many musicians will ask for funding for a new album. If you donate $10, they will send you an album once it is completed. If you donate $20, they will send you a signed album once completed. If you donate $30 they will send you a signed album and a concert ticket, and so on. If you are a new restaurant for example, you may want to offer gift cards or something of the sort for people that invest in your business and help it to come to fruition.

Equity Crowd-Funding will be arriving soon. The premise behind equity funding is similar to crowd-funding, only participants that help fund the business will own a pre-determined equity stake in the business.

Equity Financing

Different types of equity financing can consist of:

☐   Private Investors

☐   Venture Capitalists

☐   Public Offering

Private Investors, also known as "angel investors", are generally wealthy people seeking to invest in a business that will provide a greater return than conventional stocks, bonds, and mutual funds. Generally private investors will operate within the $25,000 to $2,000,000 category. They typically work with startup companies and are expecting a return of 3 to 10 times their initial investment. They often have practical experience in the industry that they are investing in.

Venture Capitalists are generally firms that invest large sums of money in companies that are already running in a profitable manner or have great potential. Venture capitalists generally invest at a minimum of $2,000,000 and up and are generally looking to return 5 to 10 times their original investment. While angel investors can have a very "hands-off" role in the operation of the company, venture capitalists frequently have a "hands-on" role in the growth and development of the companies that they have invested in. It is not uncommon for venture capitalists to have a role on the board of directors or as a key executive.

Public Offerings occur for larger, more established

companies. In a public offer, ownership stakes are sold to the general public in the form of a common stock, preferred stock, and bonds. The process of going public is a very expensive.

Preparing For A Meeting With Investors

It is crucial to not only understand the inner workings of your own business, but to also understand the industry and trends of the field you are operating within. Here is an extensive list of questions that are frequently asked by investors:

☐ What does the company do?

☐ What is unique about the company?

☐ What big problem does it solve?

☐ How big is the market opportunity?

☐ Where are your headquarters?

☐ How big can the company get?

☐ What is the market?

☐ Who are the founders and key team members?

☐ What motivates the founders?

☐ Why do users care about your product or service?

☐ What are the key differentiation features of your product or service?

☐ Who are your competitors?

☐ What gives your company a competitive advantage?

☐   What advantages do other companies have over you?

☐   What are your barriers to entry?

☐   How does the company plan to market?

☐   What is the company's social media strategy?

☐   What advertisements will be done?

☐   What are the major risks to the business?

☐   What legal risks are there?

☐   What regulatory risks are there?

☐   What product liability risks are there?

☐   What is the exit strategy?

☐   What intellectual property does the company have?

☐   What are the company's three-year financial projections?

☐   What information are those financial projections based on?

☐   How much equity and debt has the company raised?

☐   What future equity and debt will be necessary?

☐   How much of a stock option pool is being set aside for employees?

☐   When will the company be profitable?

☐   What are the factors that limit faster growth?

☐   What are the key metrics that the management team

focuses on?

- ☐ How much is being raised in this round?

- ☐ What is the company's desired pre-money valuation?

- ☐ Will existing investors participate in the round?

- ☐ What is the planned use of proceeds from this round?

- ☐ What milestones will the financing get you to?

Last but not least, be sure to research the location of the meeting, parking, and any hindrances that could possibly prevent you from getting to the meeting on time. Punctuality says a lot about how you operate your business.

Business Plan

Investors will want to see that you have thought through all aspects of your business and that you have reduced it to a Business Plan. A business plan addresses a lot of the questions that investors will be curious about. To help you develop a plan for your business, I have included this sample business plan reference for your use.

REFERENCE: BUSINESS PLAN

Sonic Management Group
Business Plan

Copy A.1

This document is for information only and is not an offering for sale of any securities of the company. Information disclosed herein should be considered proprietary and confidential. The document is the property of Sonic Management Group and may not be disclosed, distributed, or reproduced without the express written permission of Sonic Management Group.

Ben Johnson
ben@sonicmanagementgroup.com

Sonic Management Group Mission

The purpose of Sonic Management Group is to cohesively mend business with music. We seek to alleviate the musician of any business obligations so that they can focus on the craft,
which is writing, performing,
and recording music to their
full capacity. There is an influx

of quality music that is being created, but without proper representation of this content, the music is never heard or released on a large scale. Sonic Management Group's mission is to link the talent to the consumer.

Table of Contents

Executive Summary

Artists commonly face the difficult task of not only needing to align themselves with a suitable artist manager, but also to align themselves with other key industry roles such as an attorney, accountant, marketing specialist, and a graphic designer. Not only is it difficult to locate trustworthy individuals for each of these roles, but paying each individual each time a service is needed can get very expensive. The main goal in any business is to keep revenue high and expenses as low as possible.

Sonic Management Group provides artist management, and the other roles of attorney, accountant, marketing specialist, and graphic designer, all within the same company. When an artist signs on with Sonic Management Group, they automatically have access to all of the resources that will help to build and sustain a viable and profitable career. By housing all of these services within one business, Sonic Management Group will provide a cost effective solution.

Sonic will charge a 25 percent commission from all artist revenue streams. While the commission is slightly higher than that of competitors, Sonic provides services that are not provided by other companies. In the long run, a 25 percent commission will be more cost effective for the artist than having to pay freelance workers for the services that Sonic covers.

The services that are offered by Sonic Management Group include shopping music to be licensed, planning and executing live performances, music distribution, merchandising, strategic marketing, executing appearances and planning traveling logistics. Each revenue stream relies on each other in order to build the value of the overall brand. For example, when an album is recorded, Sonic will market through appropriate channels, distribute the album, produce merchandise to then sell on tour, and organize appearances to maximize the public image of the musician. Additionally, with the music that has been recorded, Sonic will seek the appropriate platforms to license the work to be used in movies, television, video games, or any other work for collaboration.

The current URL for the company is www. sonicmanagementgroup123.com. Sonic Management Group is a Limited Liability Company. President and attorney, Ben Johnson who has experience in artist management, tour management, and entertainment business consulting, owns the company. Ben Johnson currently holds an MBA from the Stanford Graduate School of Business, a Juris Doctor from the Stanford Law School, and a Bachelor of Business Administration from Stanford University.

The industry of artist management is lucrative and growing. According to the North American Industry Classification System, artist managers and agencies have

5.1% more establishments than in 2007. Additionally, revenues for these companies have increased 18.7% from 2007. By understanding industry trends and being receptive to changes in the model of the industry, Sonic Management Group will become a powerhouse organization that is sought after among artists.

The target market is modeled after a business-to-business concept. Sonic will align with an artist, which is a separate business entity. The target artist will be an 18-28 year old popular music, musician. The musician will be from an urban city and will have already amassed a loyal fan base. Making a living in music will be the musician's priority and they will not have any hindrances such as, college, a demanding job, or family obligations. Secondly, once we have built our roster, Sonic will be marketing the artists to 15-25 year old music consumers. These consumers will be urban and suburban youth that have no substantial financial obligations. They are not rich but do have enough discretionary cash to purchase a concert ticket, t-shirt, or CD. Our competitors within the market are Stampede Management, Red Light Management, and SME Entertainment.

Although Sonic Management Group has established a marketing budget, the most effective form of marketing for the company will lie in word of mouth marketing. The music industry is very small and word travels quickly as to the strengths and weaknesses of companies and individuals. Sonic will work hard to ensure that the reputation is upheld. The initial marketing budget will be used to make promotional materials (flyers, business cards, search engine optimization). Once these promotional materials are manufactured, Sonic will have the tools needed to spread the message and mission of the brand.

Sonic Management Group will be located in Orlando, Florida. Unlike many other management companies, the company will rent a 2000 square foot office. With Orlando not being a hub for entertainment, there is a budget for travel so that employees can move about the nation and the world to represent the company.

Sonic Management Group is a service-based company that relies on its intangible assets and employee brainpower. With this said, the company will not require a great amount of technology or equipment. To operate effectively, Sonic will need five MacBook computers, five iPhones, two land-line telephones, Adobe Photoshop, a projector, and Wi-Fi.

The organizational structure of the company is simple. The business manager will report directly to President, Ben Johnson. The accountant, graphic designer, and marketing specialist, will report to the business manager.

The total funds required to start this business will be $269,400. Sonic Management Group is anticipated to begin returning a profit during the third year and is projected to net $115,518 by the end of the year. A loan of $355,000 is being sought with an offer of 20 percent.

Company Description

Sonic management Group will be founded in 2018 as an artist management company. The principal place of business for Sonic is currently Orlando, Florida, however the company represents clients across America. Sonic not only specializes in artist management, but also is well versed in tour management, accounting, law, and marketing, which allows for the company to cover various facets of the entertainment business, at a low price for the client. Sonic Management Group was founded out of the sheer love and passion for music, and seeks to create viable opportunities for talented musicians. Ed Wimp and investors fund the company.

The Company's Mission

The purpose of Sonic Management Group is to cohesively mend business with music. We seek to alleviate the musician of any business obligations so that they can focus on the craft, which is writing, performing, and recording music to their full capacity. There is an influx of quality music that is being created, but without proper representation of this content, the music is never heard or released on a large scale. Sonic Management

Group's mission is to link the talent to the consumer.

Product and Services

Sonic Management Group will operate based on commission. Because of the wide variety of services that the company offers, such as legal counsel, accountants, and marketers, Sonic will be able to charge a higher commission rate than most other management companies.

The primary revenue streams that sustain Sonic Management Group are:

- Music Licensing: To films, TV shows, video games, commercials, etc...

- Live Performance: Venue tours, college tours, corporate shows, etc...

- Music Sales: Although album sales are decreasing, this will still bring in some revenue.

- Merchandise Sales

- Appearances

The revenue model identifies several income streams that will all rely on each other to increase the overall profit. For example, the artists can't do a live performance without an album released. These revenue streams will need to work in harmony in order to maximize profits. Sonic Management Group obtains revenue by earning a commission from an artist performance or appearance, or from commission from the sale of an artists CD, merchandise, license, or other product.

Development to Date

Currently, Sonic Management Group is operating under the URL www.sonicmanagementgroup123.com The website serves as a reference to contacting Sonic and provides an outline of the services offered. There are currently not any copyrights or trademarks held. The anticipated start date for the copyright and trademark will be January of 2018.

Legal Status and Ownership

Beginning in January of 2018, Sonic Management Group is an LLC with Ben Johnson as president of the company. At conception, Sonic Management Group has five employees. There are equity opportunities for investors.

Company Strengths and Strategic Position

Sonic Management Group meets the needs of consumers (musicians) by providing them with one company that can provide services to different, crucial facets of their career. Sonic will gain an advantage over other artist management companies by providing the musician with an opportunity to keep their expenses low, and their revenue high.

Industry Analysis

The NAICS code for agents and managers is 711410. There were 3,714 establishments in 2012, which was a 5.1% increase from 2007. Revenue for the industry was $5,839,000,000 which was an 18.7% increase from 2007. Total employment in the industry was 17,491, which averaged 4.7 employees per company. The average revenue for each company was $157,200,000 per year, which was a 13% increase from 2007. The average payroll per employee in 2012 was $106,921.

The music industry is rapidly being forced to change the business model. Until recently, record labels, musicians, managers, CD companies, CD distributors, and almost anyone else somehow related to the music industry, has been able to monetize through the sale of recordings. With the increase of illegal music download websites and music streaming websites, such as Spotify and Pandora, music is made available to the consumer for little, to no price. According to the article "Music Downloading: Competing Against On-Line Piracy", hip-hop is the most frequently illegally downloaded genre of music. Up to 55.8% of college aged, young men have admitted to illegally downloading music. (Music Downloading: Competing Against On-Line Piracy) It will be important to not rely on CD sales as a main source of revenue, but instead allow CD sales to complement our bigger revenue sources, such as music licensing.

I anticipate that the most profitable component of our company will be music licensing, as the licensing industry has remained relatively stable for big market films, TV shows, video games, etc...

Our market opportunity is our ability to provide professional services for a low cost. Operating as an attorney, and manager, myself, and having accountants willing to provide marketing and accounting services for commission, Sonic Management Group will be able to potentially earn the artist more money than other management companies as a result of keeping expenses low. In the long run, we hope to develop more market share for the clients signed to Sonic Management Group. When the clients succeed, we succeed. Besides licensing music, which will be profitable, we also plan to increase our presence in the market by booking more tours and TV appearances. In the long run, we plan to continue to hire young employees and interns that are knowledgeable about the current state of the music industry and we will follow any trends that we see.

Target Market

Market Description: An artist manager is an imperative component in the success of a musician. However, with the development of technology, artists are more readily able to access valuable resources on their own. Some of these resources include, marketing (social media, internet), recording, communication with industry professionals, etc... The role of the artist manager is taking effect later in the career of an artist than it has in previous times.

Managers are seeking acts that are far enough along in their careers that they are able to quickly return a profit and help create a viable venture for all parties involved. Our main competitor is a company called Stampede Management. They manage a similar genre and level of popularity of artists that Sonic Management Group will be representing. They have a solid roster of established artists and a respectable reputation within the industry. It is very likely that during the course of business for Sonic, we will have artists that work with artists from Stampede Management (touring together, collaborations on songs, appearances), so it will be important to keep a positive working relationship with them. Source: Stampede Management, http://stampedemgmt.com)

Market Size and Trends: In 1999, revenue was about 38 billion dollars and it had been decreasing every year since. In 2013, the industry had an increase of .03 percent. This percentage may not be a substantial amount but it could signify a potential plateau. (Source: Forbes, http://www.forbes.com/sites/forrester/2013/02/27/music-industry-stops-losing-money-finally/) With the industry becoming more stable, record label executives will be more likely to invest in musicians. This is good for management companies because if record labels are encouraging artists, more managers will be in demand.

Unfortunately, record sales are most likely never going to return to the revenue stream that they used to be. Therefore, record labels will feel the need to obtain revenue from the various streams that the artists and managers used to solely benefit from. This will affect our profit negatively.

Target Customers: The target is modeled by a business-to-business concept. The artist is a business entity that we are providing a service to. The artists that we will seek will primarily be 18-28 year old musicians that are deeply rooted in the music industry. Additionally, we target urban cities to scout artists that have established a positive reputation on a relatively wide scale. The artists that we acquire have the time to invest in building a successful career and are not consumed by a demanding school schedule or career, outside of performing. Furthermore, we target the consumers of the music we cultivate. Our target consumer for our product are 15-25 year old individuals that attend school and have enough discretionary cash for entertainment, such as concerts, merchandise and CD's. These consumers are not yet responsible for supporting a family or paying substantial bills. The money they earn primarily goes towards entertainment.

Competition

The music industry is competitive and risky. An artist that is incredibly talented could fail for a number of reasons that are uncontrollable. Because of this, management companies are vying over the artists that will give them the least amount of risk. It will be important for Sonic Management Group to execute a well thought out competitive analysis that will allow the company to stand out from others in the industry. The music industry currently brings in approximately 16.5 billion dollars in

revenue. (Source: New York Times, http://www.nytimes.
com/2013/02/27/technology/music-industry-records-first-
revenue-increase-since-1999.html?_r=0)

Competitors: The major three competitors that I
have researched are Stampede Management, SME
Entertainment, and Red Light Management. These three
companies have established themselves as substantial
forces within the industry.

Competitive Positions: Although these three companies
are substantial forces, they each appeal to a slightly
different demographic. Stampede Management primarily
works in the young hip-hop industry. They are reputable
and have taken a substantial market share within the hip-
hop industry. They represent eleven major artists such
as, Snoop Dogg, YG, Riff Raff, etc and a large quantity of
underground artists. (Source: Stampede Management,
http://stampedemgmt.com) Red Light Management
obtained a lot of their success by managing artists such
as Dave Matthews and Tim McGraw. They are a major
management company that has let the success of their
clients vouch for their credibility. However, even though
Red Light Management is incredibly successful, they are
not working directly in the demographic of artists that
Sonic Management Group will be working with. (Source:
Red Light Management, http://redlightmanagement.com/
about/) SME Entertainment was started by LiveNation in
1991. They not only focus on musicians, but their clients

also include athletes, keynote speakers, celebrities, and other types of public figures. (Source: SME Entertainment, http://www.smelivenation.com/about-us/) Although they are very well established, as a result of their affiliation with live nation, they cater to a lot of different kinds of markets. With Sonic Management Group specializing only in the music industry, we will have a competitive advantage.

Our main competitor, Stampede Management, has a few advantages. They have a strong grasp on the artist development market and represent the leading artists in the hip-hop industry. They have mastered the ability to cultivate artists quickly and effectively. This allows them to not have lulls in the profitability of their various talents. The weaknesses of Stampede Management lie in their inability to think "outside of the box" and come up with creative ways to package and market their artists. Their traditional view of the music industry can result in them getting left behind in the future and the industry continues to change.

Red Light Management is one of the most successful management companies in the world. Their advantages have been that they represent many chart topping artists and have established credibility by providing a grand amount of success for their artists. Their potential weakness would be that they stick to a traditional style of artist that they know will return a profit. By not taking a risk and incorporating a different style of artist into their roster, they could be missing out on a large financial gain.

SME Entertainment has a large advantage over many other management companies because they are directly affiliated with LiveNation, which owns a large share of respectable venues throughout the world. By owning and operating these venues, they have an advantage over the touring market. A weakness of SME Entertainment is that they focus on not only a wide variety of musicians, but a wide variety of celebrity personalities. Without a direct focus to a specific genre, or even a specific industry, they are not branding themselves as effectively as a company like Stampede Management, who only works with hip-hop artists.

Sonic Management Group will work exclusively with young musicians that span the genres of hip-hop, pop, and rock. The artists will collaboratively work together to build their own careers, as well as the Sonic Management Group brand. In business it is crucial to not only keep revenues high, but to also keep the expenses as low as possible. Sonic is going to provide in house legal counsel, accountants, marketers, publicists, and managers for each facet of the entertainer's career. By not having to outsource to these resources, we can keep the expenses low.

Sonic Management Group has several advantages over our competition. Some of the advantages are:
-In house accountants, legal counsel, marketing,

publicists, and managers.

-Multiple locations to be able to be more readily accessible across the country.

-Knowledge of the music industry and the various ways to create revenue.

-A creative approach and willingness to experiment with new trends.

-A network of musicians that could be brought onto the roster.

Future Competition and their Barriers to Entry: The music industry is constantly changing. Some streams are being created and other revenue streams are being eliminated. To enter into the music industry, a company must be malleable and easily able to adjust and adapt to new information and trends.

A substantial barrier to entering into the artist management industry is capital. In order to establish a professional company, money will be required. The company must have enough money to buy or lease an office, to establish the business, to invest in artists, traveling, among other expenses that are not foreseen. Additionally, the company must have a network of artists that they are confident, trust the company, and would sign with them.

Strategic Opportunities: Sonic Management Group promotes a unique asset of having in house aid from different professionals such as accountants, lawyers, marketers, publicists, and managers. Our leading competitor, Stampede Management outsources all of these tasks, which ends up putting less money in the artist's pocket. By taking a slightly higher commission than other management companies, we can earn the artist more money in the long run. Sonic Management Group will also promote the diversity and creativity that is imperative in keeping up with a fast moving industry.

Marketing and Sales Plan

Sonic Management Group plans to market through the reputation and profit that the company returns for the artists that it represents. The company strives to not only reap the financial benefits of being associated with popular entertainers, but it also strives to be an advocate for all musicians and establish business practices that will benefit all involved in the music industry.

Sonic Management Group receives an average commission of 25% of the gross revenue derived from the artists it represents. While this commission is slightly larger than that of competitors, the artist will see a higher net profit because of the drastic decrease in overhead expenses that will be incurred. Sonic Management Group will directly offer legal aid, accounting, marketing, publicity, and management to the artists that it represents. These resources are needed and can add up very quickly if there is not an in house team that can provide them. The 25%

is divided appropriately among the professionals that are involved in the success of the artist's career.

According to the New York Times, the music industry appears to be plateauing after it has been decreasing in revenue each year since 1999. In 2012 the music industry drove 16.5 billion dollars in revenue. (Source: New York Times, http://www.nytimes.com/2013/02/27/technology/music-industry-records-first-revenue-increase-since-1999.html?_r=0) With the market becoming more stable, record labels, and other industry influencers and personalities will be more comfortable investing money into artists. The industry is predicted to remain around the 16.5 billion dollar mark. However, with the new model of the industry, record labels are likely to take artist revenues from more than just album sales. Labels will likely take revenue from touring, merchandising, and any other revenue stream the artist has.

Industry professionals are finally beginning to accept the fact that the industry has changed and a different model is needed in order for everyone to profit. By launching Sonic Management Group within the next several years, the company will be able to ride the wave of new concepts and innovations that will allow music to become profitable on a large scale.

We hope to use word of mouth as our main source of marketing after we garner clients that are able to speak on our behalf. However, in the beginning we will utilize the Internet by creating a professional website that outlines our strengths. Additionally, we will implement social media to drive traffic to the website. Sonic Management Group will also create a large budget for traveling, conferences, and showcases. It will be important to meet in person with influential members of the industry and to scout for artists to work with. We will create detailed pamphlets and flyers that outline what Sonic Management Group provides, and we will hand them to people as promotional material.

In the beginning stages, the marketing budget is quite high. With a large budget, we could get a large quantity of promotional materials and create an interactive website that will represent the company well. Additionally, within the budget, we would have the opportunity to attend conferences, showcases, and travel to meet with industry professionals and potential clients. The most effective way to get marketing results is to physically speak with others in person and explain the mission of the company first hand.

Red Light Management rose to great success as a result of their affiliation with musician, Dave Matthews. Through managing top talent, the industry has gained respect for Red Light. By working hard to market the company in person, we can acquire top talent that understands the commitment we have to business and to the industry. From there, we can acquire a status similar to Red Light Management, where the quality of our talent speaks for the professionalism of Sonic Management Group.

Strategic Opportunities: With a strong legal counsel, Sonic Management Group could lobby for a higher royalty rate for streamed music. Currently, Spotify returns a royalty rate of between $.006 and $.0084 to artists that have their music on the service. (Source: Time, http://business.time.com/2013/12/03/heres-how-much-money-top-musicians-are-making-on-spotify/) This rate is very low and could potentially be raised, with the proper team to lobby on its behalf. By establishing Sonic Management Group as an advocate for the success of artists, we can increase the quality of the talent that we represent. Not only will lobbying for higher rates return us more profit in a direct manner, but it will also give us good publicity throughout the music industry.

By having in house professional services, the options are endless in the impact we can have on the well being of the music industry. Sonic Management Group plans to utilize its unique resources to establish itself as the trendsetter of the music industry.

The sales strategy will lie primarily in selling performances, CD's, merchandise, and music licensing. Sonic Management Group will make a 25 percent commission on the sales. President, Ed Wimp, or the business manager will handle the money.

Operations

Sonic Management Group is a 2000 square foot office in Orlando, Florida. While Orlando is no longer a central hub in the entertainment industry, it is still a major city that clients and industry professionals can travel to. Additionally, a lot of the work that Sonic Management Group is doing requires traveling to other cities for meetings and events.

Efficiencies: Sonic Management Group focuses on efficiently aligning tasks with competent professionals that can execute them as seamlessly as possible. The resources do not lie solely in equipment, but more in building a solid team that can aid Sonic Management Group on the path to being the best option for entertainers.

By building a team consisting of a business manager, attorney, accountant, marketing specialist and graphic designer, Sonic Management Group has the tools necessary to operate at a powerful level.

The business manager directly handles the everyday functioning of the business. This person sets up and confirms appointments, coordinates a team of interns, makes sure that all communications have been made, collects payments and disperses them appropriately, and is the interface with other companies and people.

The attorney and owner, Ben Johnson, is the face of the company and ensures that all contracts are signed, enforced, and written in the most advantageous way to all parties involved.

The accountant is responsible for making sure that the business is operating according to IRS regulations and all payments are being received and paid on time. The accountant double-checks the financial work of the business manager.

The marketing specialist is in charge of coordinating marketing campaigns. They create advertisements and establish the best means to distribute them. They work very closely with the graphic designer to manufacture appealing advertisements that represent the company and its clients well.

Sonic Management Group is a service-based business that will not require manufacturing and selling actual goods. The company will not have a return policy. However, in the event that a client or company feels as though we have not upheld our end of an agreement, we negotiate offers to re-establish the working relationship and continue to work together.

The business manager will handle any complaints and bring them to Ben Johnson's attention in order to figure out a suitable remedy.

Competitive Advantages: Sonic Management Group is established in Orlando, Florida, which gives the company an advantage with property prices. As opposed to paying top dollar for an office in New York or Los Angeles, Sonic Management Group is able to keep overhead at a reasonable price. Although it costs money to travel to other cities for meetings and events, much of the traveling expenses for events are complimentary and covered by the event itself.

The Sonic Management Group organizational structure is efficient and allows the company to offer a plethora of services to the client for a much lower price than much of the competition. Most other management companies take a commission of the gross income and pay by the hour for attorneys, accountants, graphic designers, and marketers. Sonic Management Group charges a commission of 25 percent and divide the money appropriately to all involved. The members of the Sonic Management Group staff all receive a salary.

Our goal is to establish recognition for offering a high quality service at the most reasonable price possible. By encouraging the artist as a result of returning a substantial profit, the artist will be better able to continue to produce high quality musical content.

Unlike many other management companies, Sonic Management Group operates out of an office. This will allow the company to hold meetings and invite potential clients, clients, and other industry professionals to meet with the company in a comfortable environment.

Lastly, Sonic Management Group possesses knowledge regarding all aspects of artist management. The company can advise on every aspect of the industry including touring, licensing, recording, contracts, branding, marketing and distribution.

Strategic Partnerships: The success of Sonic Management Group will rely on strategic partnerships. There will be partnerships with musicians, sponsors, events coordinators, and many other entities.

In these partnerships, both parties work in the best interest of each other and work to the fullest capacity to promote each other. Our first partnership will be obtaining talent that will represent our company well. After this partnership is established, we then begin seeking partnerships with record labels, festivals, artists to tour and collaborate with on music, hotels sponsorships, transportation services, etc.

Problems Addressed: The first issue that was raised was the issue of location. While Orlando does not have as big of a industry market as cities such as Los Angeles, New

York, Nashville and Atlanta, Sonic Management Group can establish itself in the market by use of transportation. Additionally, Sonic Management Group hopes to be a metaphorical "big fish in a small pond" by being the most well-known entertainment company in Central Florida. After establishing a strong presence in Florida, Sonic Management Group hopes to rise to becoming a "big fish in a big pond".

The use of technology (computers, e-mail, phones, skype, etc.) will aid in issue of location. Sonic Management Group will be able to meet with people across the world by using technology that is available.

Another issue is the declining revenue from CD sales. There is substantial evidence that CD sales have declined drastically with the availability of digital downloading and music streaming services. With the traditional model of selling CD's being irrelevant, it is incumbent on Sonic Management Group to strategically coordinate other streams of revenue. To fix this issue, Sonic encourages talent to perform more live shows and seek licensing opportunities. By pursuing these streams, Sonic can thrive in the new and changing music age.

Another issue is the potential of scandals that a public figure might have. For example, if Sonic Management Group is affiliated with a musician that gets caught with a lot of drugs in their tour bus, the Sonic brand could be tarnished. The company will take the preemptive measure of ensuring that all artists understand that they will be released from the company in the event of a scandal that puts our reputation at risk. It is Sonic's goal to serve as a reputable company that operates in a professional and moral manner. The company will not be affiliated with anyone or any entity that does not uphold the values of Sonic Management Group.

In order to protect the assets of the company, Sonic Management Group, the business will be covered by Hiscox Small Business Insurance (www.hiscox.com). The insurance will consist of:
   -Professional Liability Coverage
   -General Liability Coverage
   -Business Owner Insurance

Technology

Sonic Management Group relies on technology to keep accurate business records and to communicate with people around the world.

The company does not require much technology. Needs consist of the following:
   -5 MacBook Pro Computers
   -One External Hard Drive
   -Two Land-Line Telephone's
   -5 iPhone Cell Phones
   -Adobe Photoshop

-One Projector

Internet: The Internet is utilized and leveraged greatly in the success of Sonic Management Group. Not only is much communication done via the Internet, but the Internet is also our primary source of marketing in order to reach our goal of "word of mouth" marketing. The website (www.sonicmanagementgroup123.com) is promoted by exploiting "search engine optimization" capabilities. Additionally, Sonic Management Group utilizes "pay per click" optimization in order to better reach the target demographic.

Management and Organization

Key Positions: The key positions in Sonic Management Group LLC are Ben Johnson as president/attorney, and a team consisting of an accountant, marketing specialist, graphic designer, and business manager.

President, Ben Johnson holds a Bachelor of Business Administration and Political Science from Stanford University as well as an MBA from the Stanford Graduate School of Business. He also holds a Juris Doctor degree from Stanford Law School. With his knowledge and experience working in tour management and artist management, he will be capable of spearheading the effectiveness of Sonic Management Group.

Organizational Structure

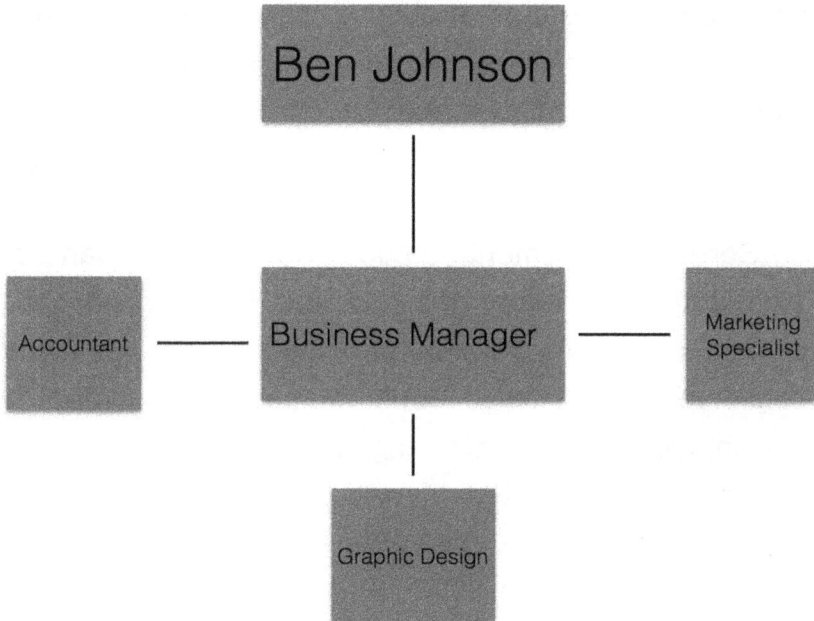

```
            ┌─────────────────┐
            │   Ben Johnson   │
            └────────┬────────┘
                     │
┌───────────┐  ┌─────┴───────────┐  ┌──────────────┐
│ Accountant├──┤ Business Manager├──┤  Marketing   │
└───────────┘  └─────┬───────────┘  │  Specialist  │
                     │              └──────────────┘
               ┌─────┴───────┐
               │Graphic Design│
               └─────────────┘
```

With the small structure of the company, there will be the opportunity for communication among all parties, however this is the structure that we will generally operate within.

Financials

Sonic Management Group will need $269,400 as the initial start-up cost for the business. The company will be based out of a rented 2000 square foot facility in Orlando, Florida. The $269,400 start-up cost will be allocated to covering remodeling, equipment, materials/supplies, and fees/professional services in order to make sure that Sonic Management Group is operating legally and effectively.

Sonic Management Group is seeking a loan for $355,000 with a return of 20 percent. Ben Johnson, the owner, is investing $50,000 of personal funds. By using conservative numbers, Sonic Management Group is anticipated to begin returning a profit during the third year of operation. It is projected that by the end of year three, Sonic Management Group will have a net profit of $115,518.

Appendix

Business Plan References

About us. (n.d.). Retrieved November 10, 2014. http://www.smelivenation.com/about-us/

Here's How Much Money Top Musicians Are Making on Spotify | TIME.com. (n.d.). Retrieved November 10, 2014. http://business.time.com/2013/12/03/heres-how-much-money-top-musicians-are-making-on-spotify/)

Music Industry Stops Losing Money, Finally. (n.d.). Retrieved November 10, 2014. http://www.forbes.com/sites/forrester/2013/02/27/music-industry-stops-losing-money-finally/

Pfanner, E. (2013, February 26). Music Industry Sales Rise, and Digital Revenue Gets the Credit. Retrieved November 10, 2014. http://www.nytimes.com/2013/02/27/technology/music-industry-records-first-revenue-increase-since-1999.html?_r=0

Red Light Management. (n.d.). Retrieved November 10, 2014. http://redlightmanagement.com/about/

Stampede Management. (n.d.). Retrieved November 10, 2014. http://stampedemgmt.com

Upshaw, D., & Babin, L. A. (2010). MUSIC DOWNLOADING: COMPETING AGAINST ONLINE PIRACY. International Journal Of Business & Public Administration, 7(1), 14-26.

The following pages contain
REFERENCE: CONTRACTS

PERSONAL MANAGEMENT CONTRACT

_____, 20_____

_____ doing business
as _____ at (location)
_____ in the State of _____
_____.

     This letter of agreement concerns your representing me as a talent and songwriter. For your services in promoting and representing me, I hereby agree to and guarantee the following:

     I. If, as a result of your efforts, I enter into a contract for my services as a recording artist with a major recording concern, I hereby agree to pay you _____ PERCENT (_____%) of any and all sales, production, or royalty advances.

        a.   A major recording concern is herein defined as a company that has gross sales in excess of one million (1,000,000) recordings annually.

        b.   You will receive an additional payment of fifteen thousand dollars ($15,000) if any album released under this agreement is certified Gold by the R.I.A.A.(Recording Industry Association of America).

     c.   You will receive an additional payment of twenty thousand dollars($20,000) above the previously mentioned payment if any album released under this agreement is certified Platinum by the R.I.A.A.

II. If, as a result of your efforts, I enter into a contract with a major management or booking concern, I agree to pay you one and one half percent (1.5%) of the gross income earned in the first two years of said agreement.

     a. A major management or booking concern is herein defined as a business which generates gross sales in excess of one million dollars ($1,000,000) annually.

III. If, as a result of your efforts, a major recording artist or company releases to the general public, one of my songs, I agree to assign FIFTY PERCENT (50%) of all publishing and copyrights to either ___(Publisher Name)__ ASCAP. or ___(Publisher Name)___ BMI. I will retain all artist and writer credits and royalties.

     a. A major recording artist is herein defined as an artist under contract to a recording concern which sells in excess of one million (1,000,000) units annually.

IV. If none of the conditions in sections I, II, and III, come into being by _____, 19___, this agreement may be made void by my written notification to you of such intent. This agreement shall remain in effect until such notification.

I hereby agree to and am bound by these terms. I set my name to this Letter the

_____ day of_____, 20____.

_____
ARTIST

STATE OF _____

COUNTY OF _____

BOOKING AGREEMENT

1.   THIS CONTRACT for the services of the music and/or entertainment described below made this ____th day of _____, 20___, between the undersigned Purchaser of music and/or entertainment (hereinafter called the Purchaser) and the undersigned Artist(s) (plus any accompanying musicians and/or entertainers) as described below, an independent contractor(s), (hereinaftercalled the "Artist").

The Purchaser hereby engages the Artist and Artist hereby agrees to perform the engagement hereinafter provided with all of the terms and conditions herein set forth including those entitled "Additional Terms and Conditions":

1. NAME OF ARTIST(S)

_____

NUMBER OF ARTIST(S) _____

2. PLACE OF ENGAGEMENT

_____

3. ADDRESS OF ENGAGEMENT

_____

4. DATE(S) OF ENGAGEMENT

_____

5. HOURS OF ENGAGEMENT

_____

LOAD IN _____

6. TYPE OF ENGAGEMENT

_____

DRESS _____

7. PRICE AGREED UPON

_____

METHOD OF PAYMENT AS FOLLOWS

DEPOSIT $ _____,
Payable to AGENT with return of contract.
        BALANCE $ _____
___, Payable to_____ in cash
immediately upon conclusion of engagement.

IN CASE OF DEFAULT BY PURCHASER: Liquidated
damages of the Artist will be the amount stated in BALANCE
in Section 7, plus reasonable attorney's fees and court costs.
    Deposit will be retained by AGENT for services performed.

8. SOUND PROVIDED BY

_____

    LIGHTS PROVIDED BY

_____

9. BREAKS: Only one 10-minute break for each hour of performance is allowed unless other arrangements are made with Purchaser.

10. GUIDELINES FOR PRIVATE PARTIES: Band members and personnel should refrain from eating or drinking on the premises of all private parties unless invited to do so by Purchaser.

No guests of Artist(s) are permitted without the consent of the Purchaser.

11. THE PURCHASER shall at all times have complete supervision, direction, and control over the services of Artist(s) on this engagement and expressly reserves the right to control the

manner, means, and details of the performance of the services by Artist as well as the ends to be accomplished. The leader shall, as agent of the Purchaser, enforce disciplinary measures for just cause, and carry out instructions as to the selection and manner of performance.

12. THE ARTIST, leader, manager, or representative of the Artist(s) _____ agrees and guarantees to pay ____ % percent of the agreed price $ _____ (Section 7 above) for personal services, booking fee, contract fee, and telephone expense rendered and incurred in this transaction to AGENT. This commission is due and payable when all parties have signed this Contract and must be paid within five days after the date that the Artist(s) is

to perform for the Purchaser except where Agent has already retained said commission from the deposit already paid by Purchaser.

If leader or key personnel of this musical group is rebooked into this or any establishment represented by the Purchaser (including chain buyers of music and/or entertainment) within 12 months from the termination of this Agreement, Purchaser and leader shall be jointly and severally liable for payment to AGENT for commission in the rate set forth in this engagement.

13. THE AGREEMENT of the Artist to perform is subject to proven detention by sickness, accidents, riots, strikes, epidemics, acts of God, or any other legitimate conditions beyond their control. If artist is unable to perform, AGENT will take reasonable measures to provide a suitable alternate Artist.

14. THIS CONTRACT constitutes the sole, complete, and binding agreement between the Artist(s) and the Purchaser. AGENT and its employees act only as agent, consultant or manager, and assumes no responsibility or liability as between the Purchaser and the Artist(s). Covenants herein contained between said Artist(s), their leader, manager or representative and AGENT are intended to be binding as between said Artist(s), their leader, manager or representative and AGENT.

15. MEMBERS OF UNIONS OR GUILDS, which may include leader and members of this unit, agree to accept sole responsibility for complying with the rules and regulations of said unions or guilds of which they may be members.

16. ADDITIONAL TERMS AND CONDITIONS

See Attached Rider if any.

_____

For PURCHASER

_____

For ARTIST

_____

(print street address)

_____

(SS # or Tax ID #)

_____

(city, state, zip)

_____

(telephone)

Contract #

_____

ARTIST PRODUCER CONTRACT

Date:_____

This   shall serve as the sole agreement between
_____ (hereinafter referred to as "Producer")
for services in producing Master Recordings, (hereinafter
referred to as "Masters") for and of the recording artist(s)
professionally known as _____ (hereinafter
referred to as "Artist").

1. The term of this agreement shall commence as of the date
hereof and shall continue until the completion of Producer's
services.

2. (a)   Recording sessions for the Masters shall be
conducted by Producer under this Agreement at such times
and places as shall be mutually designated by Artist and
Producer. All individuals rendering services in connection
with the recording of Masters shall be subject to Artist's
approval. Artist shall have the right and opportunity to have
Artists representatives attend each such recording session.
Each Master shall embody the performance by the Artist of a
single musical composition designated by the Artist, and shall
be subject to Producers approval as technically satisfactory
for the manufacture, broadcast and sale of phonorecords, and,
upon Artists request, Producer shall re-record any musical
composition or other selection   until a Master technically
satisfactory to Artist shall have been obtained, provided

additional production costs will be paid by Artist. Producer agrees to begin preproduction, rehearsals, and recording on _____, 20____ .

    (b)   Producer shall deliver to Artist a two-track stereo tape suitable for duplication and manufacture of phonorecords for each Master. All original session tapes, rough mixes and any derivatives or reproductions thereof shall also be delivered to Artist, or, at Artists election, maintained at a recording studio or other location designated by Artist, in Artists name and subject to Artists control.

3. All Masters produced hereunder, from the inception of the recording thereof, and all phonorecords and other reproductions made therefrom, together with the performances embodied therein and all copyrights therein and thereto, and all renewals and extensions thereof, shall be entirely Artists property, free of any claims whatsoever by Producer or any other person or person engaged in the production of the Masters. (It being understood that for copyright purposes Producer and all persons rendering services in connection with such Masters shall be Contractors for hire).

4. (a) Conditioned upon Producer's full and faithful performance of all the terms and provisions hereof, Artist shall pay Producer, as an advance recoupable by Artist from any and all royalties payable by Artist to Producer hereunder, the sum of $ _____ DOLLARS payable upon commencement of recording, and the balance upon the delivery to you of the Masters.

(b)   Notwithstanding anything contained in (a) above to the contrary:

(i)   in the event the Masters are released on any label other than _____
or it's subsidiary or affiliate label or labels, Producer shall not receive a royalty in connection with the sale of such records;

(ii)   in the event the Masters are released on the _____ label or a subsidiary or affiliate label, Producer shall be paid in respect to the sale of such phonorecords a royalty rate of three percent (3%) of the suggested retail price of each phonorecord sold and paid for in the United States. Payments of royalties from foreign sources shall be ONE HALF of the United States royalty rate. All fees paid to Producer hereunder shall constitute recoupable advances which shall be recouped prior to further payment of royalties.

5. Producer has agreed to assist Artist in presenting the Masters to major record companies in pursuit of a record production agreement with a major label. Producer understands that Artist will also be presenting the Masters to major labels and that Producer will not be Artists exclusive representative. Therefore, Producer agrees to notify Artist prior to making any formal contact with representatives of any major record company on Artists behalf in order to coordinate respective efforts and agrees to contact on Artists behalf only those

companies mutually agreed upon. In the event Artist enters into a record production agreement with a major label for the Masters recorded hereunder and the further services of Artist as a result of substantial efforts and negotiations by Producer with such company within the period of ONE YEAR following the completion of the Masters Artist agrees to pay Producer a commission of six percent (6%) of the actual cash advances (exclusive of recording budgets) received by Producer upon execution of said agreement. A major record company as defined herein shall be a company or corporation with gross sales of one million (1,000,000) units in the current calendar year.

6. Producer hereby warrants, represents, and agrees that he is under no disability, restriction, or other incumbency with respect to his right to execute and perform the services described in this Agreement.

7. Artist shall have the right, at Artists election, to designate other producers for recording sessions with the Artist, in which event Producer shall have no rights hereunder with respect to the Masters produced at such other recording sessions.

8. Artist shall have the right, at Artists election, to assign any of Artists rights hereunder, in whole or part, to any subsidiary, affiliated, or related company, or to any person, firm or corporation acquiring rights in the Masters produced hereunder.

9. (a) This contract sets forth the entire understanding of the parties hereto relating to the subject matter hereof. No amendment or modification of this contract shall be binding unless confirmed in writing by both parties.

(b) Artist shall not be deemed to be in breach of any of Artists obligations hereunder unless and until you have given Artist specific written notice of the nature of such breach and Artist have failed to cure such breach within thirty (30) days after Artists receipt of such notice.

(c) Nothing herein contained shall constitute a partnership or joint venture between Artist and Producer.

(d) This contract has been entered into in the State of _____, and its validity, construction, interpretation, and legal effect shall be governed by the laws of the State of _____.

(e) This contract shall not become binding and effective until signed by Artist and Producer.

_____
PRODUCER
Agreed and Accepted:

_____
ARTIST

MECHANICAL RIGHTS LICENSE

Date: _____

Gentlemen:

We control the mechanical rights in the musical work, which was not copyrighted and published prior to January 1, 1978; described below:

Title:_____

Music by:_____

Words by:_____

We hereby grant you a non-exclusive license to use the words and/or music of the said musical work substantially in their original form in the recording, manufacture and distribution of phonograph records in the United States of America, conditioned upon (1) the prompt payment to us of a royalty computed in accordance with the following schedule on each and every record manufactured, distributed or otherwise marketed by you and (2) the rendering to us of quarterly itemized statements within forty-five days of the close of each calender quarter of all such royalties so computed, accompanied by check payment of the same in full.

The royalties paid shall be 6.25¢ per side.

The word "side" as used in this agreement means one side of a disc type C.D., cassette, or the equivalent thereof having a continuous, uninterrupted playing time of not more than three and one-half minutes.

This license is non-transferable, does not convey or grant any right of public performance for profit, is limited to the recording specified below, constitutes the entire agreement between us, shall be binding upon both you and our successors, assigns and legal representatives and may be cancelled by us at any time upon your failure to pay to us the royalties provided for above.

RECORDING MASTER NO. _____

RECORD NO.   ARTIST

_____   _____

RELEASE DATE

_____

APPROVED AND AGREED TO:

Yours very truly,

BY: _____

BY: _____

MOTION PICTURE/TV-FILM SYNCHRONIZATION LICENSE

In consideration of the sum of $ _____ ,
payable on the execution and delivery hereof and upon the

agreement hereto and the acceptance hereof as indicated below, the undersigned, for and on behalf of the publisher(s) referred to herein, does hereby give and grant unto:

_____

_____

_____

the non-exclusive, irrevocable right and license to record the following copyrighted musical composition(s) in synchronism or timed-relation with a single episode, program or motion picture made and produced solely for television purposes by the said licensee and now entitled:

TITLE   WRITERS
PUBLISHER   USE

_____

_____

_____

_____

_____

_____

_____

Subject to the following terms and conditions:

This license is granted upon the express condition that the said recording(s) are to be used solely in synchronism or timed relation with said television-film, that no sound records produced pursuant to their license are to be manufactured, sold, licensed or used separately or apart from the said television-film, and upon the further condition that the said television film shall not be exhibited in or televised into theaters or other public places of amusement where motion pictures are customarily shown or places where an admission is charged.

This is a license to record only, and the exercise of the recording rights herein granted is conditioned upon the performance of said musical composition(s) over television stations having valid licenses from the person, firm, corporation or other entity having the legal right to issue performance right licenses on behalf of the owner of such rights in the respective territories in which said musical composition(s) shall be performed hereunder, or for the United States from the owner thereof. However, the said recording(s) may not be performed by means of so-called "pay" or "subscription" television, or by means of audio visual devices or contrivances such "EVR" or any method or devise similar or analogous there to or otherwise used except in the performance thereof originating from and as actually broadcast by a television station.

This license is granted for the territory of:_____

_____

The term of this license shall be for the period of ___

_____ years from the date hereof, and upon such termination any and all rights given and granted hereunder shall forthwith cease and terminate, including the right to make or authorize any use or distribution whatsoever of said recording(s) of said musical composition(s) in said television-film otherwise.

This license cannot be transferred or assigned by affirmative act or by operation of law, without the express consent of the undersigned in writing.

The undersigned warrants that said publisher(s) are the owners of the recording rights herein licensed, and this license is given without other warranty or recourse, except for their agreement to repay the consideration paid hereunder in respect of any of said musical compositions, if said warranty shall be breached with respect thereto, with the liability for breach of said warranty being limited in any event to the amount of the consideration paid hereunder; with respect to such musical compositions: and the undersigned reserves all rights and uses whatsoever in and to the said musical composition(s) not herein specifically granted.

City:_____

State:_____

Dated:_____

AGREED TO AND ACCEPTED:

_____

By: _____

POPULAR SONGWRITER'S CONTRACT

AGREEMENT entered into this _____ day of __
_____ 20____, by and between _____
_____ herein designated as the
PUBLISHER, and _____
_____ author and/or composer, hereinafter jointly designated
as the COMPOSER.

WITNESSETH:

1. The COMPOSER hereby sells, assigns, transfers and delivers to the PUBLISHER, its successors and assigns, the original musical composition written and composed by _____
at present entitled _____
_____ which title may be changed by the PUBLISHER; including the title, words and music thereof, and all rights therein, and all copyrights and the rights to secure copyrights and any extensions and renewals of copyrights in the same and in any arrangements and adaptations thereof, throughout the world; and any and all other rights that the COMPOSER now has or to which he may be entitled or that he hereafter could or might secure with respect to this composition, if these presents had not been made, throughout the world; and to have and to hold the same absolutely unto the PUBLISHER its successors and assigns.

2. The COMPOSER hereby convenants, represents and warrants that the composition hereby sold is an original

work and that neither said work nor any part thereof infringes upon the title of the literary or musical property or the copyright in any other work, and that he is the sole writer and composer and the sole owner thereof and of all the rights therein, and has not sold, assigned, set over, transferred, hypothecated or mortgaged any right, title or interest in or to the said composition or any part thereof, or any of the rights herein conveyed, and that he has not made or entered into any contract or contracts with any other person, firm or corporation whomsoever, affecting said composition or any right, title or interest therein, or in the copyright thereof, and that no person, firm or corporation other than the COMPOSER has or has had claims, or has claimed any right, title or interest in or to said work or any part thereof or any use thereof or any copyright therein, and that said work has never been published, and that the Composer has full right, power and authority to make this present instrument of sale and transfer.

   3. In consideration of this agreement, the PUBLISHER agrees to pay the COMPOSER as follows:

   (a) An advance of _____ is hand paid, receipt of which is hereby acknowledged; or any other sum heretofore or hereafter advanced to the COMPOSER, which total sums shall be deductible from any payments hereafter becoming due to the COMPOSER under this agreement.

   (b) A royalty of _____ cents per copy on all regular piano copies sold and paid for in the United

States of America.

(c) A royalty of _____ cents per copy on any form of orchestration thereof sold and paid for in the United States of America.

(d) A royalty of _____ for each use of the lyrics and music together, in any song book, song sheet, folio or similar publication containing at least five musical compositions.

(e) For purposes of royalty statements, if a composition is printed and published in the United States, as to copies and rights sold in Dominion of Canada, revenue therefrom shall be considered as of domestic origin. If, however, the composition is printed by a party other than the PUBLISHER in the Dominion of Canada, revenue therefrom shall be considered as originating in a foreign country.

(f) An amount equal to _____% of all net receipts of the PUBLISHER in respect of any license issued authorizing the manufacture of the parts of instruments serving to mechanically reproduce the said composition, or to use the said composition in synchronization with sound motion pictures, or to reproduce it upon so called "electrical transcriptions" for broadcasting purposes; and of any and all net receipts of the PUBLISHER from any other source or right now known or which may hereafter come into existence.

(g) A royalty of _____% of all net sums received by the PUBLISHER on regular piano copies and/or orchestrations thereof, and for the use of said composition in any folio or composite work, sold and paid for in any foreign country.

(h) In the event that the said Composition shall not now have lyrics, and lyrics are added to the said composition, the above royalties shall be divided equally between the COMPOSER and the other writers and composers.

4. It is specifically understood and agreed that the intention of this agreement is not, and the COMPOSER shall not be entitled to receive any part of the monies received by the PUBLISHER from the American Society of Composers, Authors and Publishers, or any other performance right society from which the PUBLISHER shall receive payments for the use of said musical composition in all countries of the world.

5. It is agreed that no royalties are to be paid for professional copies, copies disposed of as new issues, copies distributed for advertising purposes, or lyrics or music separately printed in any folio, book, newspaper, song sheet, lyric folio or magazine, or any other periodical, except as above set forth. It is also distinctly understood that no royalties are payable on consigned copies unless paid for, and not until such time as an accounting therefor can properly be made.

6. The PUBLISHER agrees that it will render to the COMPOSER semi-annually on or about the 15th day of February and August of each year, a statement showing all sales showing all sales and royalties earned by the said

COMPOSER to the preceding December 31st and June 30th and will pay to him at the same time all royalties then due and owing.

7.   The COMPOSER hereby expressly grants and conveys to the PUBLISHER the copyright of the aforesaid composition, with renewals, and with the right to copyright and renew the same, and the right to secure all copyrights and renewals of copyright and any and all rights therein that the COMPOSER may at any time be entitled to, and agrees to sign any and all other papers which may be required to effectuate this agreement. And the COMPOSER does hereby Irrevocably authorize and appoint the PUBLISHER, its successors or assigns, his attorneys and representatives in their name or in his name to take and do such actions, deeds and things and make, sign, execute, acknowledge and deliver all such documents as may from time to time be necessary to secure the renewals and extensions of the copyright in the aforesaid composition, and to assign to the PUBLISHER, its successors and assigns, said renewal copyrights and all rights therein for the term of such renewals and extensions and the COMPOSER agrees upon the expiration of the first term of any copyright in the aforesaid composition in this or in any contract, to do, make, execute, acknowledge and deliver, or to procure the due execution, acknowledgement and delivery to the PUBLISHER, of all papers necessary in order to secure to it the renewals and extension of all copyrights in said compositions and all rights therein for the terms of such renewals and extensions.

8. The PUBLISHER agrees to publish the said musical composition in saleable form within one year after the receipt of lead sheet of the said composition. Should it fail to do so, the COMPOSER shall have the right, in writing, by registered mail, to demand the return of such unpublished composition, whereupon the PUBLISHER must within sixty days after receipt of such notice either publish the said composition, in which event this agreement shall remain in full force and effect, or upon failure so to publish, all rights of any and every nature granted to the PUBLISHER herein in connection with the said unpublished composition shall revert to and become the property of the COMPOSER and shall be reassigned to him.

In connection with the foregoing it is distinctly understood and agreed that if the PUBLISHER shall secure a commercial phonograph recording, or an electrical transcription, or, a synchronization in a motion picture, of the said composition; such recording, transcription or synchronization shall, for the purposes of this agreement, be deemed publication by the PUBLISHER.

9. The COMPOSER agrees that he will not transfer nor assign this agreement nor any interest therein nor any sums that may be or become due hereunder without the written consent of the PUBLISHER first hereon endorsed, and no purported assignment or transfer in violation of this restriction shall be valid to pass any interest to the assignee or transferee.

10.   The COMPOSER hereby authorized the

PUBLISHER at its absolute discretion and at the COMPOSER'S sole expense to employ attorneys and to institute or defend any action or proceeding and to take any other proper steps to protect the right, title and interest of the PUBLISHER in and to the above entitled composition and every portion thereof acquired from the COMPOSER pursuant to the terms hereof and in that connection to settle, compromise or in any other manner dispose of any matter, claim, action, or proceeding and to satisfy any judgement that may be rendered and all of the expense so incurred and other sums so paid by the PUBLISHER the COMPOSER hereby agrees to pay to the PUBLISHER on demand, further authorizing the PUBLISHER, whenever in its opinion its right, title or interest to any of the writer's composition are questioned or there is a breach of any of the covenants, warranties or representations contained in this contract or in any other similar contract heretofore or hereafter entered into between the PUBLISHER and the COMPOSER, to withhold any and.all royalties that may be or become due to the COMPOSER pursuant to all such contracts until such question shall have been settled or such breach repaired, and to apply such royalties to the repayment of all sums due to the PUBLISHER hereunder.

11. The term COMPOSER shall be understood to include all the authors and composers of the musical composition above referred to. If there be more than one, the covenants herein contained shall be deemed to be both joint and several on the part of the writers and composers and the royalties hereinabove specified to be paid to the

COMPOSER, shall, unless a different division of royalty be specified, be due to all the writers and composers collectively, to he paid by the PUBLISHER, in equal shares to each. This agreement may be executed by writers and composers in several counterparts.

12. All questions and differences whatsoever which may at any time hereafter arise between the parties hereto touching these presents or the subject matter thereof, or arising out of or in relation thereto, and whether as to construction or otherwise, may be referred to arbitration under the provisions and the supervision of the American Arbitration Association.

13. This agreement contains the entire understanding between the parties, and all of its terms, conditions and covenants shall be binding upon and shall inure to the benefit of the respective parties and their heirs, successors and assigns. No modification or waiver hereunder shall be valid unless the same is in writing and is signed by the parties hereto.

IN WITNESS WHEREOF, the parties hereto have executed this agreement the day and year first above written.

_____   By _____

WITNESS

_____   Composer _____

WITNESS   Address _____

_____ Composer _____

WITNESS Address _____

_____ Composer _____

WITNESS Address _____

_____ Publisher _____

WITNESS Address _____

_____

SPONSORSHIP CONTRACT

AGREEMENT made this _____ day of _____, 20____. by and between AGENCY __ _____ and _____, (hereinafter referred to as "SPONSOR").

It is mutually agreed by and between all parties as follows:

1. The SPONSOR agrees to present the following performances upon all the terms and conditions hereinafter set forth, and agrees to do so upon such terms and conditions:

       A.   Artist or Attraction:

       B.   Theater or Place(s) of Engagement:

       C.   Date(s) & Time(s) of Performance:

       D.   Date(s) & Time(s) of Rehearsal:

2. It is agreed that as full compensation for the services mentioned herein, the SPONSOR will pay to _____ _____ or specified delegate in United States currency, or acceptable bank draft the designate sum of:

_____

       A.   Payments will be made to _____

_____

B.   Method of payment: Fee is to be delivered to:

_____

Immediately after completion of the scheduled performance

3. SPONSOR agrees to furnish at its own expense for each performance and rehearsal, the Theater or place(s) of engagement, properly heated, ventilated, lighted, clean, in good order and

adequately staffed. SPONSOR warrants and represents that SPONSOR is at the present time, or will be the owner or operator of, or has or will have a valid lease upon the place(s) of engagement covering the date or dates of the above engagement and that SPONSOR has or will have the right to present the engagement provided for herein at such place(s) of engagement.

4. SPONSOR agrees to furnish at its own expense the following:

_____

_____

_____

_____

_____

5. SPONSOR shall furnish at its sole cost and expense, all items (except those items which AGENCY herein specifically agrees to furnish and pay for), including, but, not limited to, ushers,

ticket sellers and all other box office employees required for advance and single ticket sales, ticket takers, all licenses, tickets, bill posting, mailing and distribution of circulars, publicity services of every type required for the proper fulfillment of the engagement.

6. SPONSOR agrees to pay for all charges including, but not limited to, stage hands, stage carpenters, electricians, sound technicians, truck loaders and unloaders and any other local labor as shall be necessary and/or required for the performance.

7. SPONSOR shall have sole and exclusive control over the production, presentation and performance of the engagement hereunder including, but not limited to, the details, means and methods of Performance of the said engagement and the Performances of each participant therein, and the persons to be employed by SPONSOR in performing the provisions of this engagement.

8. The Agreement cannot be assigned or transferred without the prior written consent of SPONSOR. The agreement represents the full understanding between the parties and neither party shall be bound by any terms or undertakings until executed by SPONSOR. The terms AGENCY and SPONSOR are used herein shall include and apply to the singular and plural and to all genders. The Agreement shall be construed and the legal relations between the parties determined in accordance with the laws of the state of _____
STATE_____. AGENCY agrees to hold SPONSOR

harmless for any and all claims arising out of this agreement and/or its performance, including, but not limited to, attorney's fees.

9. AGENCY agrees to furnish _____ copies of a black & white photograph, _____ color photographs, and a biography of the performer(s) by _____. AGENCY also agrees to provide the suggested music with titles, credits, names of composers which performer(s) wishes to perform on the program by ____ _____.

10. AGENCY represents that ARTIST/ATTRACTION will arrive at all performances and or rehearsals on time and will furnish at its sole cost and expense any costumes, clothing, shoes, props, food, makeup, hairstyles, musical instruments and/or any other items relating to the ability of the performers to perform successfully (except those items specified in this contract as to be provided for by the SPONSOR).

11. AGENCY agrees to disburse the agreed upon compensation for services mentioned in paragraph 2, to the ARTIST/ATTRACTION as agreed upon between AGENCY and ARTIST/ATTRACTION. SPONSOR is held harmless from any and all compensations for services by the AGENCY and ARTIST/ATTRACTION, except as specified in this contract.

12. In the event that one or more of the members of the production cannot perform because of ill health, physical disability or other reasons beyond his/her control, AGENCY shall use its best efforts to furnish a substitute of similar stature for such member of the Production whom SPONSOR agrees to accept. SPONSOR does not have to accept any substitutes provided by the AGENCY, but, may contract a substitute of their own.

13. AGENCY grants SPONSOR permission to tape, record, film, broadcast the concert and/or rehearsal without additional compensation for services to AGENCY or ARTIST/ ATTRACTION for Television broadcast and commercial release.

14. In the event that the Performance of any of the covenants of this agreement on the part of SPONSOR shall be prevented by act of God, physical disability, the acts and regulations of

public authorities, or labor unions, labor difficulties, strike, civil tumult, war, epidemic, interruption or delay or transportation service or any cause beyond their or its reasonable control, SPONSOR and AGENCY shall be respectively relieved of their obligations hereunder with respect to the Performance(s) so prevented. In the above mentioned event AGENCY grants SPONSOR the right to reschedule the performance(s) under the same terms and conditions of this contract.

15. The SPONSOR shall have the option to suspend or cancel said agreement if it has not been duly signed and returned to:

_____

_____

_____

16. By his execution hereof, the person executing this instrument on behalf of ARTIST/ATTRACTION individually represents and warrants that he is fully empowered to bind ARTIST/ATTRACTION hereunder by specific authority of the individual, body or group having control of the business affairs and contractual commitments of ARTIST/ATTRACTION.

This agreement (including _____ riders attached hereto) constitutes the entire understanding between the parties, supersedes all prior understandings, and cannot be changed, except by

an instrument in writing signed by the SPONSOR and AGENCY.

AGREED TO AND ACCEPTED:

_____   _____

SPONSOR   AGENCY

_____

ARTIST

ARTIST TECH RIDER

1. ARTIST'S Requirements Are as follows:

2. PRESENTER agrees to provide the following:

a. Suitable and appropriate hall for the performance of the ARTIST. Rooms, hallways and stage shall be cleaned to the satisfaction of the ARTIST or ARTIST'S representative.

b. At least _____ separate changing rooms adequate for up to _____ performers.

c. Technical staff necessary for set-ups, strikes (including light and stage arrangements), and run of show as specified in technical requirements. Additionally, all facilities shall be staffed as may be necessary for all activities including concession sales, plus staffed for the performances.

d. Tickets, sales of tickets and all front of house personnel; all advance publicity including announcements, mailings and printed performance programs. Presenters are to return all unused materials immediately after performance.

e. Access to performance space(s) and crew the entire day of performance, plus adequate rehearsal time preceding performance in the same space and with the same crew, plus a full technical rehearsal prior to the performance. Lighting focus shall be completed _____ in advance of performance.

f. Theater / performance space ground plans and instrument

/ equipment inventory _____ weeks prior to ARTIST'S arrival; equipment necessary to all or any activities of performance / residency as listed in technical requirements. Details of such needs to be sent with other stage and technical requirements (See TECHNICAL REQUIREMENTS).

g. A hot meal (_____ _____) after sound check on the day of performance for ARTIST. Also, bottled water for each artist during performance.

h. A conspicuous location where ARTIST's merchandising can be sold, including _____ standard table and _____ chairs.

i. Parking spaces, validation or coverage for performers and technical staff, if needed.

j. All lodging for performers and technical staff .

k. Upon request, a minimum of _____ ( ) complimentary tickets to said performance.

3) ARTIST agrees to provide the following:

a. Press kits including photographs, articles, reviews and program copy.

b. Program copy supplied shall be reproduced in full and exactly as offered to the PRESENTER in all printed programs. All references to the ARTIST in paid or unpaid advertising, announcements, house boards, flyers, posters, publicity releases and any other promotional materials for the service (s) above shall be as follows:

Name of Artist _____

The ARTIST shall have the right to alter the performance program sent to the PRESENTER at any time up to and including the performance.

c. Availability for newspaper, magazine, radio and television interviews as desired by PRESENTER, if logistically feasible.

TECHNICAL REQUIREMENTS (to be furnished by PRESENTER):

a. STAGE: Requirements for stage are a minimum of _____ feet wide by _____ feet deep of flat surface, without any obstruction (such as, but not limited to nails, broken floor boards, electrical outlets, poles, wires). All flooring, masking and hanging / circuiting / patching of light plot will be completed before arrival of ARTIST.

b. FLOOR: All nails and staples must be removed, holes filled or taped and unused floor pockets covered. The floor and wings must be clean, and swept, prior to rehearsal and performance.

c. LIGHTING: ARTIST carries no lighting equipment. It is mutually understood that a light plot for the individual theater will be formulated by the PRESENTER, and that the PRESENTER's technical staff will take care of all lighting design, hanging and loading in for this event. It is also mutually understood that all lighting design and technical aspects of this event must receive prior approval of ARTIST.

   d. SOUND: ARTIST carries no sound equipment. PRESENTER must provide a first class sound system that includes:

   1. _____ main house amplifier (s) of ____ wattage each

   2. house speaker system including

   _____

   3. _____ ( ) downstage stage monitor speakers

   4. separate mixer for monitors:

   5. _____ ( ) microphones and stands: _____ vocal mics; _____ boom stands, _____

   regular _____ percussion mics on boom stands.

   6. headset intercom system with stations for the Stage Manager, Electrician (s), Sound Technician, Follow Spot Operator and Curtain Man

   7. _____ reverb and delay units for vocal mics

   8. mixing board with _____ inputs and technician, plus technician for monitors on stage with reverb available.

   9. _____ direct boxes

e. STAGEHANDS: This is not a yellow card attraction. Stagehands may be non-union unless local regulations require that union people be employed.

PRESENTER agrees to employ and pay all stagehands, whether union or non-union, including loaders, if required. Stagehands must be the same people for both rehearsal and performance.

1. Technical Director with working knowledge of facility and with authority to represent PRESENTER to act as assistant to the Stage Manager at all times.

2. Stagehands (number to be determined by Technical Director) are required to work the set-up prior to ARTIST arrival and four ( ) are required for rehearsal and performance as follows:

- monitor technician on stage - "guitar" technician to assist guitarist during show (can be a staff tech) - deck technician (may double as spot operator) - light board operator (and assistant if necessary) -sound technician for front of house

f. DRESSING ROOMS: The PRESENTER will provide _____ ( ) clean, private dressing rooms, one for _____ and the other _____ for up to _____ band members, and not allowing public access to the performance area. Each room must have make-up lights and mirrors, chairs and tables, costume rack, nearby lavatory and sink, and be close to the stage. The PRESENTER must also supply

_____, bottled water, and healthy snacks. In addition, the dressing rooms are to be heated or cooled to the ARTIST's satisfaction.

g. REHEARSAL SPACE: Stage must be available for sound check and rehearsal three (3) hours prior to showtime.

General References

1. *How Much Does TuneCore Cost? What Is the Price of Music Distribution & Publishing Administration?* Tunecore, 8 Jan. 2013. Web. 10 June 2016.

2. "Record Sales: Where Does the Money Go?" Record Sales: Where Does the Money Go? Bandzoogle, 9 June 2006. Web. 10 June 2016.

3. "Scripting Must Be Enabled to Use This Site." How Much Does TuneCore Cost? What Is the Price of Music Distribution & Publishing Administration? Tunecore, 8 Jan. 2013. Web. 10 June 2016.

4. Fonteney, Eric De. "Why Release a Digital Only-Album?" Why Release a Digital Only-Album? Music Biz Academy, 1 Aug. 2005. Web. 10 June 2016.

5. Shambro, Joe. "Wanna Be a Rock Star? Here's How to Sell Your Music on ITunes." About.com Tech. N.p., n.d. Web. 10 June 2016.

6. Price, Jeff. "The More Money Spotify Makes, The Less Artists Get Paid... - Digital Music News." Digital Music News. Digital Music News, 12 June 2015. Web. 10 June 2016.

7. Koedooder, Margriet. "Margriet Koedooder." HOW MUSIC LICENSING WORKS. N.p., n.d. Web. 10 June 2016.

8. Zarronandia, Jeff. "Judge Rules That." Snopes. Snopes, 22 Sept. 2015. Web. 10 June 2016.

9. Robley, Chris. "What Is a Mechanical Royalty?: Music Publishing Royalties Explained." DIY Musician Blog. CD Baby, 25 Apr. 2016. Web. 10 June 2016.

10. Goldmacher, Cliff. "Five Things Songwriters Can Do To Move Their Careers Forward." BMI.com. BMI, 28 Sept. 2011. Web. 10 June 2016.

11. ASCAP, BMI & SESAC: What's The Difference?" Songtrust. Songtrust, 21 May 2015. Web. 10 June 2016.

All contracts were provided by Hip Hop Production, LLC

Performing live concerts and selling merchandise are not the only ways to build a career. Within the pages of this comprehensive book, author Ed Wimp shares practical, usable information about ways to make money in the music business, while garnering fans and building your brand.

Ed Wimp is a musician. He has worked as a Road Manager and Artist Manger with International Touring Artists. Ed holds a Bachelor's Degree in Business Administration, a Master's Degree in Entertainment Business and is currently pursuing a law degree. Ed has seen the music business from all sides and has created this easy-to understand guide to put you on the path to fulfilling your dreams.

Building Fans, Fame and Wealth: The 18 Revenue Streams of Music is a useful tool for any musician, artist manager, or industry professional looking to increase their income in the music business. This book provides real life examples of viable revenue streams, and demonstrates ways to implement them into your career.

www.edwimp.com

.

www.ingramcontent.com/pod-product-compliance
Lightning Source LLC
LaVergne TN
LVHW011234080426
835509LV00005B/487